A SUSSEX GUIDE

THE COUNTY OF SUSSEX

ENGLISH CHANNEL

GATWICK
EAST GRINSTEAD
RYE
HORSHAM
HAYWARDS HEATH
HASTINGS
HEATHFIELD
MIDHURST
BRIGHTON
LEWES
EASTBOURNE
CHICHESTER
WORTHING
A23
A272
A265
A27
A259

THE SHAPING OF
THE SUSSEX
LANDSCAPE

PETER BRANDON

INTRODUCED BY
LORD DENIS HEALEY

Illustrated by
GRAHAME BAKER SMITH

SNAKE RIVER PRESS

SNAKE RIVER PRESS

Book No 17
Books about Sussex for the enthusiast

Published in 2009 by
SNAKE RIVER PRESS
South Downs Way, Alfriston, Sussex BN26 5XW
www.snakeriverpress.co.uk

ISBN 978-1-906022-16-7

This book was conceived, designed and produced by
SNAKE RIVER PRESS

ART DIRECTOR & PUBLISHER *Peter Bridgewater*
EDITORIAL DIRECTOR *Viv Croot*
EDITOR *Robert Yarham*
PAGE MAKEUP *Richard Constable & Chris Morris*
ILLUSTRATOR *Grahame Baker Smith*
CONSULTANT *Lorraine Harrison*

This book is typeset in Perpetua & Gill Sans,
two fonts designed by Eric Gill

Printed and bound in China

DEDICATION

*To the memory of Hilaire Belloc who first aroused
in the author his love of Sussex*

CONTENTS

FOREWORD

I am not a native of Sussex. I was born and raised in that other fine county, Yorkshire. Over 25 years ago, my wife Edna and I came to live in Sussex, just outside the village of Alfriston. Our house looks down to the Channel at Cuckmere Haven, and from the top of our garden we have a beautiful view over the village itself, where the Clergy House was the first acquisition of the National Trust, bought by Octavia Hill over a century ago for only £10.

I have always seen our Sussex home as my earthly paradise as have many others who have come to the county: Virginia and Leonard Woolf at Rodmell, Vanessa Bell and the Bloomsbury group at Charleston, Rudyard Kipling at Rottingdean and Burwash to name but a few; it was Kipling who captured the beauty of 'our blunt, bowheaded, whale-backed Downs' in four lines:

> Bare sloped, where chasing shadows skim
> And through the gaps revealed,
> Belt upon belt, the wooded, dim
> Blue goodness of the Weald.

What makes Sussex so attractive is its infinite variety. It has coast, with both sand and pebbles, high chalky cliffs, low-lying salt marshes, the High Weald, woodland, heathland, forest and Downs, all packed into 934,900 acres. Peter Brandon's book, wearing its erudition and experience lightly, shows us how our beautiful landscape was forged, by nature and by the fortitude, hard work and plain old obstinacy of generations of Sussex natives from Neolithic times onward; he also shows us how we can learn to 'read' it, to develop an historical eye for the telling detail that indicates that here was an iron smelting plant, there they ploughed with oxen, this was the main sheep route. All we have to do it is take a leisurely walk – in any direction – and take the time to observe, and trace the patterns left by layers of history. As he says, 'every acre has something to reveal' and this book will help you find it.

LORD DENIS HEALEY

INTRODUCTION

'No other county has such treasure
As ours in overflowing measure ...'

E. V. LUCAS

Two agencies shape a landscape: nature and man. Nature prescribes the lie of the land, the form of mountains, hills, valleys and streams, climate and natural vegetation, and largely determines soils. Man can only modify nature to a limited extent but, over millennia, he has repeatedly transformed the 'wild' or natural environment according to his changing needs as civilisation has evolved from that of the hunter-gatherer to the sophisticated urbanisation of the present day. Woodland has been grubbed up, heathland eradicated and marshes drained, to make room for farms, factories, harbours, places of leisure, villages and towns up to the hugeness of monstrous cities. Sussex has 2,000 years of recorded history but its occupation by man goes back half a million years. Thus Sussex conveys the feeling of a very old country, full of an extraordinary wealth of visible features.

Almost everyone who has ever lived, married and died in that enormous space of time has left no word of what their daily lives were like, what was happening in the world around them, or of their love affairs, sport, crimes, illnesses and changes in fortune – in fact the sorts of things that occupy the waking hours of most men and women. But 'ordinary' people over time who have, for example, cleared a wood or laid out fields and streets have left an indelible legacy on the landscape or townscape whenever they have built or in any way, however small, changed their environment. Our forebears have left their mark by repeatedly building and rebuilding and reshaping landscape. Past inhabitants have had the power to reshape their surroundings to a remarkable degree and from the marks they leave on the ground in the present landscape we can infer something of their lives. This makes the actual history of the landscape so fascinating. How *did* the walls, hedges, ditches, roads, canals come into existence, and when, why and by whom?

Such man-made changes are invariably never totally complete: parts of the former landscape tend to survive because they were still regarded as useful, if only in a rather altered form, and therefore the present face of an historic landscape of an English county like Sussex is a mixture of buildings, fields, town streets and settlements of different ages, purposes and origins. This medley has been likened to a palimpsest, a Greek manuscript on which two or more texts have been written, each being partly erased to find room for the next. Thus in the landscape of today successive generations of inhabitants at a particular place are likely to have played some part in creating its present-day appearance. This means that the past is not over and done with, but is alive and in the present.

Historic landscapes that have continually evolved over a long period of time have a peculiar fascination of their own for they have something special about them, an ancient feeling full of 'treasures' – the picturesque villages and country towns, castles, ruined abbeys, old churches, country houses, historic parks and gardens, Saxon 'camps' and older 'forts' and 'rings'. There is an extraordinary wealth of associations, architectural, historical and literary. Every acre has some secret to reveal.

Moreover, the locality tends to have a special distinctiveness which marks it out from neighbouring places, so giving a much needed variety and sense of place in our ever-growing, uniformly built world. In addition to showing what they look like, historic landscapes or townscapes also tell us what the present inhabitants feel about their locality and how they are protecting it to retain its individuality and distinctiveness. What emerges from this are the remarkable differences between places in Sussex and how they came into being and evolved into their present distinguished and mellow character. Gathering knowledge of the imprint of fields, woods, hedges, ponds, farmhouses, trackways and urban streets and houses that shaped the landscape for centuries and gave it meaning reminds us how easily it can be erased by modern technology in a single day, and once gone it cannot be restored, unlike the habitat of the skylark. It is our one enduring asset and our home. Its study gives meaning to the need to cherish and look after a place and to make permanent changes only after the deepest consideration.

There is still a vast amount to be discovered from the man-made landscape, especially in woodland which hides everything made earlier. Furthermore, the visual evidence of the imprint of some known features is still puzzling and there is room for reinterpretation of others. So everyone with eyes to see, an inquisitive mind and a modicum of knowledge can contribute to the history of any particular place.

Acquiring an 'historical eye'

A variety of techniques is used to discover the history of Sussex from the land itself. Walking the ground, whether in the countryside or the town, is the most important and basic approach of all. On the Downs and heaths, walking in the winter season when the sites are less obscured with fern and bramble, or when the fields are ploughed or unsown, is the best time; it is better in summer for the marshes such as the Pevensey Levels or Amberley Wild Brooks, when they are drier.

But walking is of no use unless one is seeing, as distinct from looking, and seeing with an 'historical eye'. Acquiring this, and cultivating it, is a matter of practice. A beginner will take time to train his or her eye to see things historically in the landscape for they are often so small and subtle that they are either normally ignored or taken for granted, such as a former cottage which has survived only as a derelict, briar-covered garden; the faint, partially ploughed-out traces of a track going across fields; an old, broken-down mill dam; the base of a windmill; or the tell-tale touches on a building which give a clue to its date. It will take rather longer to see the landscape with the eyes of its former occupants, from the standpoint of their needs and capacities. An experienced walker-historian will find that he can draw on more senses than sight. Even the soles of one's feet are an invaluable help, for instance, in the detection of the slightly undulating surface of a pasture – proof of earlier ploughing; and a good depth of leaf mould felt through the feet will tell the experienced walker of a landscape buried out of sight beneath him. This recreation of the past can only be partial. We cannot hope to bring back fully the countryman's ordinary day, for we see it incompletely in a kind of looking glass.

Tools for the job

Apart from a good camera, possibly binoculars, stout shoes or boots and weatherproof clothing, the choice of a map is crucial to an understanding of countryside or town. For the latter, an accurate plan at different stages of growth is indispensable. For the country, Ordnance Survey maps are essential. The 1-inch map (where 1 inch represented 1 mile) was long in standard use but it does not show the amount of detail possible on the larger scale of the current Explorer 1:25,000 maps (roughly 2½ inches to 1 mile, or 4 cm to 1 km), and this is now the best map for all outdoor activities. A larger scale, such as the 6-inch map is useful for a small area but it will not extend over a large enough area to reveal the general run of the country. An enthusiast for studying the past on the ground will eventually want to turn to the County Record Offices and similar repositories of local history, to search for documents relating to what he has seen on the ground.

Before setting off

It is worth stressing that the field walker will probably find that his landscape under study was utterly different 150 years ago. The houses in a downland village that one now admires were once farmsteads or farm cottages, BMWs are all that are now housed in former barns and there is not a pig in the street. In the High Weald of Sussex there is abundant evidence of man's former activity – quarries, pits, ponds, mounds of waste at every turn, and hints of woodcrafts, but all around now is silence and it is sometimes hard to find anyone to talk to. The rural exodus to London and the towns from the 1860s has swept away almost the entire population of country people who once worked in this countryside, often leaving not a single trace of their cottages which simply fell down. In many cases what we have now in this former industrialised landscape is a playground – a manicured estate for a city gentleman. The author has just found a classical temple erected over old brick pits and stone quarries; there are many similar surprises awaiting. Happy hunting! There is so much to do and little that is so rewarding in a county so naturally and historically endearing.

A GEOLOGICAL MOSAIC

SUSSEX BEFORE MAN

A characteristic of Sussex is its extraordinary natural diversity due to its underlying geology. Gilbert White of Selborne distinguished no less than six different strips of soil below the northern scarp of the chalk in his single parish and this applies also to every parish similarly located in Sussex. In the hilly part of the Weald ('The High Weald') the soils vary between neighbouring farms and even within a farm. A geological or soil map does not do justice to them. In addition, Sussex has sea, cliffs, Downs, woods, hills, marsh and heath and a geology which is an intricate mixture of old sea bed, chalk, sand, sand-stone and clay. This has yielded a mosaic of Downs and Weald, sea cliffs, shingle beaches, rich plains, winding river valleys, arable pasture and woodland and ragged heath culminating in fold after fold rising to Ashdown Forest. Each of these different rocks produces a distinctive flora and wildlife and in the past shaped farming activities.

It is consequently difficult to find anywhere in the world an area of comparable size which exhibits so perfectly the response of plant, animal and human life to this diversity. This has made for a remarkable local distinctiveness , for whatever became the local building material for the village – flint, sandstone or clay – influenced differences in farming and building styles. Sussex is indeed a land of miniatures, seemingly all the world in a few square miles, and all this is accessible by means of one of the densest networks of public rights of way in England.

Much of the fascination of the historical evolution of Sussex is due to the contrast between the centre and the fringes. Three clear-cut and sharply distinct districts, each wearing different faces, are the coastal plain of West Sussex, the South Downs and the Weald. Each supported in the past, more than they do now, distinct economies and rural cultures. This was largely because of differences in soil. The soils permeate the whole of economic and social history and as the human landscape that developed on each soil type tended to be shaped by people of different backgrounds, speech and folklore, the human occupation and subsequent economic development proceeded in different ways and at different rates. The trade in products between these contrasting, but complementary, districts is the origin of the road pattern which is generally north-south and not east-west.

The coastal plain

Although the coastal plain is now heavily built over, there are still remaining areas of unspoilt shingle, as at Camber and Shoreham, which are probably as near to wilderness as any in England. Behind these, the plain is some of the most naturally fertile soil in Europe interspersed with wide inlets known as 'rifes'. Before drainage and reclamation during the Middle Ages it must have reminded Saxons of their homeland across the North Sea. Still further behind are successive former shorelines marked by 'raised beaches' which were the habitat of the prehistoric hunter-gatherer.

The Downs

Proceeding northwards are the utterly different worlds of the South Downs and the Weald. On the Downs local conditions meant that sheep farming was the blood and soul of the region for more than 5000 years, and the representative peasant was the shepherd. It was a hard land from which to make a living without sheep, for not only did sheep provide meat, wool, tallow, skins, etc., but the cultivation of corn on the thin soils was impossible without their manure. It is difficult to realise that thin and easily eroded chalk soil was the cradle of Sussex. From *c.*4000 BC to *c.* AD 1200 it was the Downlanders who 'ran' the whole of the rest of Sussex because the densest population lived on the Downs and on or near them were the headquarters of the elite. 'Sheep and corn farming' sums it up over 6,000 years until 1940 when ploughing up in wartime and during the austere post-war years transformed the Downs to their present state almost overnight.

The Weald

The Weald, a former wilderness on indifferent soils, was a small-scale people's landscape created by a combination of hard work, mutual support and an element of stubbornness, a world of the small family farmer and the self-sufficient smallholder, cottager and squatter. Their lives revolved around woodlands and the representative peasant was the forester, either concerned with the management of oak or the harvester (coppicer) of hazel or Spanish chestnut, now largely a thing of the past, and the farmer-artisan, the man who supplemented his meagre living from the soil with handicrafts, and who has also gone into oblivion.

This most singular landscape, culminating in Ashdown Forest with its air of Yorkshire moorland, has never been as profoundly humanised as most of the English countryside. This is because in a region of unresponsive soils the farmer has never driven the land hard. It was land hunger on the Downs and coast that drove people into the Weald from the 12th to the 14th century and their clearance of the woodland is a human achievement without parallel in medieval England, making the Weald a human epic as well as a natural marvel.

The extensive woodland and heath, which existed before it was domesticated by medieval peasant farmers, still lingers as an enormous patchwork of little fields bordered by thick hedges and hedgerow timber, little copses, woodland glades and endless scrubby bits. It's ribboned with a labyrinth of green lanes and narrow byways with wide verges, but an extraordinary lack of main roads. This densely wooded region, stretching by wooded fold to wooded fold into the blue distance can, from some vantage point on high ground, still give an illusion of the former Forest of the Andredesweald, always seen from a distance, but never reached. It remains one of the most extensively wooded districts in England, a land hidden from the rest of the county, and even from itself, for the woods and high-banked hollow ways conceal farms and hamlets buried in deep valleys separate from each other, and so it provides endless surprises.

The Weald is divided into two: the Low Weald and the High Weald, the former wrapping round the other like a girdle. This has unforgiving cold clay soils. According to Sackville-West of Sissinghurst, the Wealden farmer was 'a wrestler who broke the unkindly spirit of the clay in battle and plodded over it in a steady and unhurrying gait until the clay crept into his bones before its due time'. Sussex clay indeed does weed out all but the hardest working farmer, the toughest of foresters, the most dogged of huntsmen, and the least timid of walkers. The Wealdsman tended to be of a different temperament from the Downsman, being more independent and resourceful and a rather rugged individualist who was nonconformist in religion, who could be, and occasionally was, rebellious and whose watchwords were, 'We won't be druv'.

The western Weald abutting on to Hampshire and Surrey is built of varying rocks comprising clays, sands and sandstones. It is a country-side of infinite variety where a tumble of green hills, coppices and woods, commons, meadows and arable melt into one another with springs and brooks embedded in the remains of heaths, which were once wide-spread, to form an exceptionally lovely and lovable landscape.

Stone & marble

In a clay country like the Weald every wealthy house-builder cried out for 'Horsham Stone', a flaggy sandstone, to 'heal' the roof. This is one of the most delightful building stones in England. It is impervious to rain and weathers beautifully to green and orange tints because it is hospitable to lichen. 'Sussex Marble' or 'Petworth Marble', a conglomerate of freshwater molluscs taking a fine polish, was used for more ornate pillars, fonts and altars in churches and for mantelpieces in farm- and country houses. Of varied local sandstones dug for building, the loveliest is golden sandstone streaked with ruddy iron staining.

Chalk was usually too soft to be a successful building material but it is found as 'clunch' in the walls of barns, wherever eaves could protect it from the weather, and for the interior of downland churches. More generally used, and accounting for much of the charm of a downland village, is flint, the characteristic building material of chalk country.

The human landscape

This, then, is the stage which was shaped by the farmer, woodman, ironmaster, potter, fisherman and seaman. We shall spend much time with them, for in the past most people worked on the land or at sea. But we shall need to consider the people who moved into Sussex from London and the towns from the beginning of the Railway Age, and who totally transformed the county, especially along the coast, bringing with them urban habits which changed rural ways of life for good. Sussex has had a compelling fascination for the *nouveaux riches*, the weekender and the family who wanted to escape from the stress and rush of living in London. To Victorians and Edwardians the Weald and the Downs lay as a survival of an older England, with customs, manners and dialect a hundred years or more behind 'progressive' parts of the country. In the 18th century this, and the muddiness of the roads, made the Weald about as welcoming as Afghanistan is today. But to an urban escapee from monstrous London, the largest city in the world in 1900, the Downs and Weald were as scenes of deepest Arcadia, with an air of withdrawal, privacy, intimacy and permanence, a kind of hidden world, almost a fortress, freeing them from business and noise.

Top Places

◗ *Poling Church, near Littlehampton, for the 'feel' of the coastal plain, or Apuldram, near Chichester in the Selsey peninsula*

◗ *Houghton and a walk along the River Arun for a glimpse of the Downs*

◗ *Milland parish church and adjacent redundant Saxon church*

TAMING THE COUNTY

HUNTERS & FIRST FARMERS

The earliest humans we know of were nomadic hunters who roamed Sussex during spells of warmer weather during inter-glacials in the last Ice Age. As a result of excavations in gravel pits at Boxgrove we know that more than 400,000 years ago, in a now-buried landscape, hunters based along the line of the existing shoreline could use tools crafted from the flint nodules from the sea cliffs to hunt their prey skilfully and butcher it competently. They were already humans in total command of their patch, which implies generations of inherited training and considerable organisational ability. They were far from the 'savages' that people were once taught to believe at school and university. Further investigation of the raised beaches along the coastal plain, including Brighton, would probably produce other centres of hunting activity.

Post-glacial hunter-gatherers

About 11000 BC signs of climatic change appeared, first with the coming of birch and aspen followed successively, as temperatures rose, by pine and hazel, alder and oak, lime and elm, holly, beech, hornbeam and maple. By 5500 BC natural woodland, termed the 'Wildwood' by Oliver Rackham, covered almost all Sussex in varying density. So it was from the woodland that Sussex people had their earliest beginnings and to survive they had to clear it.

The first post-glacial hunter-gatherers were Mesolithic peoples who had highly distinctive implements which included microliths – small, finely worked blades of flint used as projectiles – axe-like pieces and scrapers. The owners of these tools lived in rudimentary structures for their winter quarters, mainly on the present sandy heathlands, as at Selmeston near Lewes, and in rock shelters when hunting in summer in the Weald at Tilgate Wood, West Hoathly, High Hammerwood, Buxted and High Rocks near Groombridge.

Farmers & miners

The earliest farmers are well represented on the South Downs. The Sussex flint mines appear to be the earliest in England, beginning about 4000 BC at Harrow Hill above Worthing, Blackpatch, Church Hill and Long Down, followed later by Cissbury. These were mined until about c.2800 BC and highly valued axes were bartered along the South Downs Way. These flint mines thus represent the earliest resource exploited by man in Sussex. Men termed Neolithic easily worked the hard glassy substance of flint into any desired shape or form. By chipping off slivers, known as flakes, and using another stone or piece of antler as a hammer, a piece of flint would be shaped into a robust implement such as an axe. Alternatively it could be made into cutting tools or shaped into knives, scrapers and arrow tips.

Six causewayed enclosures of the period have been identified on the Downs whose function is unclear. Three are large: Belle Tout near Eastbourne, the inner parts of Whitehawk above Brighton, and the Trundle near Chichester. The elite were buried communally in earth-built long barrows, e.g. Bevis's Thumb at Compton above Chichester.

The Bronze Age

During the Bronze Age (c.1500-500 BC) woodland clearance and farming seem to have spread all over the Downs. Today, with the new knowledge acquired from the technique of pollen analysis, there is much more that can be learned about the settlement, farming activities and social organisation of this period. This is partly explained by the fact that the contemporary landscape is often buried under a sheet of downwash loosened by the ploughing of steep hillsides above. The most distinctive feature is the round barrow, or circular burial mound, which contained an individual and usually grave goods. Settlements now number 26 in the Middle Bronze period alone, including sites at Plumpton Plain, Itford Hill and Black Patch. The Itford site, excavated by Peter Drewett, disclosed a number of circular huts, each with a large central post and with smaller ones placed equidistant around the perimeter. The roofs would have been made with boughs and roughly thatched, and the walls probably lined with wattle and daub. There were paddocks for cattle and the whole site was remarkably like African villages today. In the larger huts, storage pits were dug deep into the chalk, the gashes made by bronze axes still clearly seen. Carbonised barley was found, in one hut, presumably grown on the small irregular fields on sloping ground marked by cultivation banks known as lynchets. Trackways entered from outside and there are 11 round barrows in the vicinity. The late Bronze Age landscape at Shinewater in the Willingdon levels near Eastbourne is one of the most exciting discoveries in recent years.

The Iron Age

During the Iron Age, woodland clearance on the Downs went on apace to cope with the expanding population and was virtually completed on the eastern South Downs, which attained their familiar bare outlines so cherished today. The most obvious features on the landscape are the hillforts. Many had their origin between c.450-75 BC and this is true of Cissbury, the Trundle above Chichester, and Mount Caburn near Lewes, which have impressive ramparts. Recently their defensive function has been considered to be mixed with other cultural needs. By the beginning of the first century AD each block of downland demarcated by a river valley seems to have had a hillfort replacing many of the older forts. These have feebler defences such as Torberry, Thundersbarrow, the Devil's Dyke, Butser Hill and Bow Hill.

The stage that farming had reached is well exemplified by the unique project in Britain set up by Dr Peter Reynolds in 1972 known as Butser

Ancient Farm, which was later transferred to Chalton. Here a working farm was reconstructed as it would have been in about 300 BC, with livestock, crops and equipment as nearly as possible the same as the originals. It is an open-air research laboratory, open to the general public. Suffice it to say that Peter Reynolds transformed most persons' ideas of Iron Age peoples and of their achievements. Many have come to believe that the circular thatched house could well have lasted longer than the likely span of our current semi-detacheds; that the coppicing of hazel for fencing was then known, as were the beneficial effects of sowing legumes for nitrogen alternately with wheat, both innovations confidently thought until recently to be late Saxon or post-Norman developments; and that with an ard (*see p.23*), and not a plough, it was possible to produce surprisingly large yields of corn. Some claim that when milled and made into flour, the Emmer and Spelt wheat sown was higher in protein, richer in vitamins and tastier than modern bread wheats.

Looking for clues

Broadly speaking, anything that breaks the smooth slopes of the Downs, whether it is a hollow or a mound, a dimpled surface, a bank, however subtle, or a shallow line, is likely to be man-made and therefore worthy of investigation. Bracken is often another sign of past human activity as it is rampant on ground enriched by manure. Scrubby patches invariably betoken listed archaeological sites on which ploughing is forbidden. The best times for field walking are either very early in the day or late in the evening when long shadows throw up clearly any break of slope.

The most striking features on the present landscape of farming activity in the Bronze, Iron and Romano-British Ages are the cultivation banks called lynchets which divided the small regular-shaped fields. The origin of these was long disputed; William Cobbett, for example, thought they had been dug with a spade. In actuality they seem to have arisen from a natural process developing over time: the downward shift of soil from a ploughed field to one below due to rain, snow and frost. A bank on the lower side of a field became ever higher with the loosening of soil above it – a positive lynchet – and the bank below also grew in height as soil was washed away from it – a negative lynchet. Good examples are Buckland Bank, near Falmer, and the slopes of Chantry Hill near Sullington.

Although most of the lynchets were bulldozed in the farming revolution during and after the last war, they are still identifiable to a surprising degree by their soil and crop marks. The bands of darker and lighter soil which are apparent on a newly ploughed field indicate respectively the humus or topsoil which accumulated above a lynchet and the remains of the chalk exposed on the bare slopes between lynchets. Crop marks will help determine lynchets, for corn growing on the remains of a positive lynchet will probably stand taller on the humus and deeper soil and be correspondingly a little shorter on the remains of a negative lynchet. These stored-up patterns are most visible from high ground overlooking extensive ploughed land in autumn.

We now take our leave of prehistoric Sussex. What in imagination can we see and hear in the Downs on the eve of the Roman invasion in AD 43? It was George Holleyman's study of aerial photographs in 1935 that first revealed a densely farmed landscape laid out in blocks of little square fields (Celtic fields) within closely spaced settlements of varying sizes and forms, including single farms and villages, some being as little as a mile apart. An important element in the distributions on Holleyman's map is that people were packed closely together on the optimal sites of gently sloping spurs on the middle and lower slopes of the Downs, which had good soil and accessible water for cattle. The upper slopes and crests were sheep runs. This was a pattern to last for nearly another 2,000 years.

Top Places

◈ Walk from the car park on Chantry Hill near Storrington out on the Downs to Harrow Hill and Black Patch, the site of former flint mines

◈ Highdown, near Worthing, Cissbury Hill, Chanctonbury Ring and The Trundle near Chichester, fortified enclosures

◈ 'Barrow hunting' in the western South Downs on Heyshott Down (at least ten); the bell barrows known as the Devil's Jumps on Treyford Down and the 'King's Graves' barrows on Bow Hill overlooking the Kingley Vale National Nature Reserve

VILLAS, ROADS & RUINS

ROMANO-BRITISH SUSSEX

In recent years a controversy has arisen about the invasion beachhead for the Roman invasion of Britain in AD 43. Doubts have been cast on the traditional account that the Romans landed at Richborough in Kent, in favour of a landing along the Solent. This is in the light of the archaeological work undertaken at Fishbourne near Chichester, since the 1960s, which indicates considerable pre-invasion Romanisation in the heart of the pro-Roman chieftain Verica's territory. What Sir Barry Cunliffe unearthed at Fishbourne between 1961 and 1968 was the most important discovery in Romano-British archaeology in the previous half century. It was a huge and well-constructed masonry build-ing that lasted into the third century, earlier than any previously found in Britain, luxuriously appointed, including seven floor mosaics and a great formal garden which is unequalled west of Italy. So far, nothing has been found in Britain to compare with it in magnificence. The site was presumably a palace, built initially AD 75-c. 80 for Tiberius Claudius Togidubnus, who, as a client king, was responsible for the government of the surrounding area. Only now are we appreciating the complexity of the landscape of which the palace is a part.

Desirable villas

Fishbourne was a grander version of a number of villas which arose in the area following the Roman invasion, including Bignor, Pulborough,

Angmering, Southwick, Brighton, Beddingham, Barcombe, Newhaven and Eastbourne. Each of them had some form of underfloor heating and their occupants enjoyed a leisurely and elaborate form of bathing. Villas were the residences built on larger and more productive farms than those of the peasants, and appear to have been owned by a landowning aristocracy. Their presence below the Downs or on the coast may suggest that they were the headquarters of estates that extended deep into the Downs and probably also northwards into the Weald.

Settlements, villages & farms

Numerous Romano-British villages have also been identified. Houses built of timber, wattle and daub on a rectangular plan replaced the circular Iron Age dwellings. Some had glazed windows and locks, a clear sign of affluence. Fields were ploughed with a more efficient type of ard (a plough which does not turn over the sod) and specially constructed corn-drying kilns have been discovered at several sites such as Thundersbarrow, on the Downs near Shoreham, and around West Blatchington near Brighton. At Bishopstone and Bullocks Down near Eastbourne were long-lived farms in an organised mixed-farming landscape.

Roman roads

What everyone knows about the Romans is their impressive road build-ing ability. I.D. Margary's *Roman Ways in the Weald* (1948) is a masterly account of his detective work before World War II, which led to the rediscovery of long stretches of Roman road in Sussex, previously lost for centuries. With the aid of his clearly mapped routes based on 6-inch Ordnance Survey maps, it is possible to follow on foot parts of Stane Street over the Downs, for example, or to take a length of the London-Lewes Way from Holtye to Hartfield in the Weald. The latter contains a formerly excavated section, now turfed over again to protect the metalling made up of cinders from nearby ironworks. The wheel marks, presumably from Roman chariots and carts, were clearly visible in a surface compacted as hard as concrete.

The iron industry

Iron was manufactured on a large scale in Roman Sussex. Largely based on ore at the base of the Wadhurst Clay, it was worked soon after the invasion in the Hastings-Sedlescombe area. By the mid 2nd century the industry appears to have moved to between East Grinstead and Wadhurst. Here it survived until the mid 3rd century when over-exploitation may explain why the industry moved on to the Forest of Dean. The ore was roasted in small furnaces or bloomeries, so called from the spongy 'bloom' of iron which cooled from the molten slag. At Beauport Park in Hastings, fragments of tile at iron-working sites bear the monogram of the British fleet, CL BR, i.e. CLASSIS BRITANNICA.

Decline & fortification

From the late 3rd century the eastern and southern parts of the Roman province of Britain came increasingly under barbarian attack. Chains of forts were built along the coasts of Gaul and Britain to act as naval bases. Portchester Castle was built *c.*280 and Pevensey Castle (Anderida) about 50 years later. The walls of Chichester were strengthened with bastions on which a garrison would have mounted catapults.

The worsening attacks on Britain and the rest of the Roman Empire led to the withdrawal of Roman armies in Britain in 383 and 407. The official break from Rome appears to have been in 410 when local communities were told to organise their own defences. The most dramatic entry in the *Anglo-Saxon Chronicle*, compiled during Alfred's reign, reads under the year 491:

> In this year Aelle and Cissa besieged Andredescaster (Pevensey Fort), and killed all who were inside, and there was not even a single Briton left alive.

Top Places

❯ *Bignor Roman Villa, close to the Roman road from Chichester to London, is an archaeological jewel with remarkably fine mosaics*

❯ *Fishbourne Palace*

❯ *The outer walls of Pevensey Castle*

❯ *The Romano-British field system at Buckland Bank near Lewes*

THE SOUTH SAXONS ARRIVE

THE GERMANIC INVADERS

The Kingdom of the South Saxons was the most important consequence for Sussex of the invasion by barbaric tribes from across the North Sea in the 5th and 6th centuries AD. Although the smallest of the independent Anglo-Saxon states, its very name *Sud Sex* in the Saxon dialect (the land of the South Saxons) gave an identity to Sussex and a feeling of separateness and provincialism that it has not even now entirely lost.

It is no longer thought that the invaders drove away or massacred most of the Romanised Britons. Instead of dispossessing them, the conquerors are reckoned, at least in some cases, to have infiltrated the inhabitants who remained on their own land, much like the peasantry after the Norman conquest. Recent place-name study seems to confirm this.

Nevertheless, the old economy appears to have collapsed completely and reverted probably to something like the prehistoric way of life before the Roman occupation – even in the 4th century urban life appears to have been effectively dead. Rookery Hill, on a spur of downland overlooking Bishopstone near Seaford, is one of the few early Saxon settlements to have been excavated. A group of 22 huts, including three sunken ones, all timber buildings of varying size, were found there. It was from these small and crude beginnings that Sussex began its development anew, this time under Saxon influence.

The grain of the country

Examining the Explorer OS sheet 136 of part of the High Weald southeast of, for example, the area around Stonegate, near Burwash, provides a casual impression of the typical humpy, hilly country with its surviving chequerboard of little hedged fields, determined by natural features, such as incised streams, gullies, hillsides and woods that have never been cleared. But a more thorough study of the map reveals that this is but half the story. Instead of the expected random pattern of fields and lanes guided solely by natural features, the whole landscape has had a grid superimposed on it by some human agency, with a particular grain running roughly north-northeast to south-southwest. Almost every feature in the landscape straddling the River Rother conforms to this general pattern – the twiddly lanes, bridleways, footpaths, the fields, boundaries of farms and woods, and also the church and village of Stonegate. Assuming that the grid is evidence of the direction followed by the main movements of early people, then it is a sign that the Burwash area of East Sussex was colonised by Jutes from adjoining Kent in the 6th and 7th centuries following the Germanic invasions. This is consistent with what is known about the cultural origin of the whole area in the hinterland of Hastings.

Such a gridded landscape is found in other parts of the Sussex Weald, as well as in Surrey and Kent, e.g. in the Horsham district where the grain is roughly north to south, i.e. between the South Downs and the Low Weald. The grid, as in the Burwash district, has been formed by sub-parallel droveways from the Downs and coast which originally connected manors in the south of the Kingdom of the South Saxons with their swine pastures and timber-gathering grounds in the Weald to the north. Stretches of these droveways, which characteristically are 30 feet (10 metres) or more wide, are metalled and used today as highways; other parts have disappeared; yet others are delightful greenways, ribbons of fauna and flora, which can magically transport you back to the days of Shakespeare and Chaucer. Another fine set of north-south droveways is in the Lewes-Eastbourne district from whence they ran into the Weald up to Heathfield and nearby places some 10 to 15 miles (16 to 24 km) away. It is extraordinary that these fundamental features of the Wealden landscape have never been thoroughly investigated and mapped. Any interested person who walks into the country with open eyes can add some contribution to our knowledge of this matter. The pattern is less obvious where fast-running streams have dissected the landscape, as around Mayfield.

Saxon worship

The history of Christianity in Sussex effectively begins with St Wilfrid's mission in the 680s, which led to the founding of the See of Selsey that ended in 1070 when William the Conqueror transferred it to Chichester. Of particular interest is the substantial proportion of churches containing surviving features of Anglo-Saxon workmanship. H.M. and J. Taylor's list of Anglo-Saxon churches in England numbers 267, of which 18 and possibly more are on the Downs. Ecclesiastical historian E.A. Fisher regarded the 'probables' of Taylor as certainties and added 20 more. The great disparity between these two figures arises from the difficulty of dating precisely many of the ancient churches.

At Jevington, Sullington and Singleton, Saxon west towers survive. Sompting, with its Saxon tower of about the same date, is one of the most famous Anglo-Saxon churches and the only surviving example of a steeple of the 'helm' type derived from churches in the Rhineland. Bishopstone, one of the early minster churches, had a Porticus, or side chamber, used for special services. The first little churches had normally a single or a double chamber. A few existing churches retain the simple single-cell structure to this day, including East Marden, North Marden and Didling, Wiggonholt, Buncton, Denton and West Dean near Eastbourne. Tiny, and rather later, two-cell churches are relatively common and include Chithurst, St Botolph's Hardham, St Peter's Westhampnett, Greatham, Up Marden (with one of the loveliest interiors in England) and Selham. Several of these ancient churches are on, or adjacent to, burial mounds raised imposingly by pre-Christians, e.g. Hamsey, Piddinghoe, Southease, Tarring Neville and Berwick.

A number of these modest little churches have remarkable works of art in the form of early wall paintings. These comprise the most famous in Britain and their survival is largely attributable to the relatively unrestored condition of churches of parishes which became impoverished with the fall in population in the later Middle Ages. The most complex paintings are at Plumpton, Clayton, Coombes and Hardham. It has been suggested that the paintings might be as early as the late Saxon period, although the consensus appears to be that they fall within the period $c.1100\text{-}1150$, a period known as the 'Saxon overlap'.

The origin of the Sussex village

One of the still unresolved questions about Saxon Sussex is the origin of the villages which are such an attractive feature of the present scene. This issue is related to another question: 'When and why were the Downs emptied of their substantial earlier farming population?' In 1978 Barry Cunliffe remarked that a systematic campaign of intensive field survey and excavation would undoubtedly advance our understanding, but little work has been done in the past 30 years. Cunliffe himself suggested a possible model based on his studies at Catherington just across the Hampshire border. After walking the ploughed fields washed by rain he searched systematically for characteristic pottery of the early Saxon period. This technique yielded a number of new settlement sites, including substantial village sites on the High Downs. These discoveries, and the hilltop site of Rookery Hill (*see p.25*), suggest that the old notion that the earliest Saxons settled in valleys is no longer tenable.

The possibility, following Cunliffe's study, is that a number of small downland settlements were abandoned by the 9th century for larger ones on the richer soils in the downland valleys and at the spring line below the scarp slope. Applying Cunliffe's model to Sussex, Up Marden and Compton in West Sussex occupy hilltop sites similar to neighbouring Catherington in Hampshire, which could conceivably have been 'mother' sites of early occupation subsequently left rather isolated by a later migration down to the valleys. What is clear is that a shift of population in the 9th and 10th centuries swept away most of the population from the High Downs to spring-line villages. Presumably peasants at these places had farms along the village street and strips of land in the common fields from which they worked the sheepwalk. The actual site of a specific village appears to have been controlled to some extent by a convenient spring, but because many scarp-foot villages lie almost equidistant, i.e. between Bepton and Harting, there is the possibility that their parish boundaries were inherited from Romano-British estates. A number of these places are found in the Domesday Book.

Rural life

From the 9th century the rural structure of Sussex, with the exception of that of the Weald, evolved into a pattern which lasted up to the 16th century and beyond in some respects. Peasants lived in village streets at small farmsteads. Their small flocks of sheep were pastured in common on the Downs by day and brought down on to their dispersed strips of arable in the common fields around the village at night. Meadows in the river valleys were also shared in common. Their cattle were pastured on another shared resource, the common. Their pigs were driven into the Weald in summer until the 14th century. The Lord of the manor owned his own sheepwalk, meadows and arable independently of the peasants and although he owned the common he did not pasture animals there.

Enclosure of the common fields began as early as the 15th century and was largely complete by 1700 though scraps persisted until later and some parishes, such as Amberley, kept the traditional structure until the early 19th century. Most commons were enclosed by Acts of Parliament during the 19th century. Timeline Historical Maps taken from 1-inch Ordnance Survey maps published between 1805 and 1874 show former commons and other signs of the rural structure. Boundary banks normally divided distinctly different land usages, and detailed study on the ground of a particular parish, together with early topographical maps, will throw up evidence to reproduce the surroundings with which past villagers were familiar.

Town planning

The creation of towns seems to have started only from the 10th century. One clue to this is the absence of pagan burials at Chichester and Hastings and the lack of coin-find spots at centres which later became urbanised. Chichester was organised for trade, defence and refuge against the Danes by 894 when it became a fortified *burh* during Alfred's reign. The intra-mural street, which is today such an attractive feature of the city walls, was designed for the military purpose of providing access to the garrison troops defending the walls. Four other places were set up as *burhs* roughly equidistant from one another: Burpham, Lewes, Hastings and *Eorpeburnam* in the extreme east of Sussex. These were intended to shelter refugees fleeing from invasion. Lewes and Hastings grew into towns; Burpham has been left empty on the Downs since the Roger of Montgomery founded Arundel on the opposite side of the River Arun. *Eorpeburnam* , another abandoned place, has been identified as the site of Castle Toll in Newenden, now just across into Kent. Lewes was set out at the foot of a promontory spur, strongly defended on three sides by natural features – marsh, river, ravine and steep slopes.

In the reign of Athelstan, in the 10th century, a place with a mint making coins is evidence of trade. Lewes emerges with two mints, and Hastings and Chichester with one each. (Canterbury had seven, Rochester had three.) Steyning grew into a minor site with its own mint later. This embryonic urbanism illustrates the overwhelming rural character of Saxon Sussex.

Top Places

- *Highdown, above Worthing, an early Saxon site, refortified against the Danes in the 9th century*
- *Burpham, good specimen of a surviving Saxon* burh *on the River Arun, abandoned in the 11th century*
- *The Mardens churches on the Sussex-Hampshire border*

WILLIAM OF HASTINGS

THE NORMANS

Apart from the Industrial Revolution, England has never experienced such a shake-up as that resulting from the aftermath of the Battle of Hastings on October 14th 1066. The Normans clearly demonstrated their technological superiority in warfare and between the morning and evening of a single day sealed the fate of England with an iron hand. Kipling said England was '*hammered into line*', one of his most felicitous phrases in '*The Anvil*'.

Sussex experienced some of the greatest changes for it was the heartland of William the Conqueror's arch-enemy Harold, King of England, and potentially vulnerable to further invasion. William concentrated Sussex into the hands of his close relatives and most loyal supporters in the form of a military occupation. The Saxon administrative divisions, called rapes, were reorganised as power bases, each with a castle at their centre and a port. These comprised Hastings (headed by Robert, Count of Eu), Pevensey (Robert, Count of Mortain), Lewes (William de Warenne), Bramber (William de Braose) and Chichester and Arundel (Roger of Montgomery). Another administrative change was the so-called rape of Battle Abbey, a circular estate with a 3-mile (4.8-km) radius created by William as a war memorial around the site of the Abbey, which he founded on the battlefield of Hastings. Each of the Norman rapal lords confiscated all the landholdings of the Saxon elite and allocated them as manors to their triumphant knights.

A number of new towns arose including Arundel in the shadow of its castle, Shoreham as a new port at the mouth of the River Adur, and Battle, the initiative of the Abbey. New market towns also developed with increasing trade, such as Uckfield.

Monks, abbots & priors

The Saxon Church was drastically brought into line with the Norman model. The cathedral of the diocese was transferred from Selsey to Chichester to conform with the siting of cathedrals in towns. Monasteries became the centre of renewed religious life. William's own foundation, Battle Abbey, was followed by William and Gundrada de Warenne, co-founders of the great Cluniac Priory of St Pancras at Lewes in 1077. On the coast a prodigious outburst of new church building began in the Romanesque style as at Steyning and Old and New Shoreham.

In cultural respects the Normans made much of Sussex less a part of England than an outlier of Normandy in the 12th and early 13th centuries. This influence was greatly strengthened by the habit of the early Norman lords of creating priories and cells as dependencies of Norman or other European monasteries. The plan of the church of Lewes Priory was based on the third church at Cluny, its mother house. The collegiate church at Steyning, one of the finest specimens of 12th-century architecture, was built under the supervision of the monks of Fécamp and its nave has a strong resemblance to the Romanesque churches of northern France. The churches of Old and New Shoreham (the latter was intended to be collegiate) and Boxgrove Priory, established as a cell of Lessay Abbey in 1117, have a striking similarity of design to that of Lessay Abbey itself, so remarkably that Boxgrove church was a template for the restoration of Lessay Abbey, after it was destroyed during World War II.

The religious fervour of the 12th century is most notably marked by the endowment of the great Benedictine abbey of Battle, the high altar of which William insisted should be placed on the very spot where King Harold fell. The surviving Norman remains comprise part of the dormitory, cloister walls and undercrofts of the guesthouses. The founding monks came from Marmoutier on the Loire. Abbot Ralph greatly enlarged and embellished the abbey from 1101-24 and its rounded apse, ambulatory and radiating chapels were to be repeated at Canterbury and other cathedrals. The building of the Abbey was achieved only with difficulty, for the King's insistence that it should be built on the site of the battlefield meant that crypts and cellars had to be dug into the narrow hilltop and the creation of earthen platforms were necessary.

At Lewes, William de Warrenne and his wife Gundrada jointly founded the Priory of St Pancras in 1077. This was placed under the direct control of the Burgundian house of Cluny – then a fount of art and learning in Europe and the centre of monastic reform – which resulted in elaborate liturgy, chant and prestigious architecture. The church was larger and more richly ornamented than Chichester Cathedral and even today the Priory ruins, though mere fragments of their former magnificence, are impressive enough to convey something of the scale and grandeur of the buildings achieved by the 13th century. The church was almost completely razed to the ground but the *hospitum*, now part of the parish church of Southover, and the remains of the infirmary chapel still exist. Both the founders were originally interred in the chapter house of the Priory. Subsequently their bones were placed in two little lead coffers. Since the discovery of William de Warenne's coffer when the railway from Brighton to Lewes was under construction in 1845, his and his wife's remains are now housed in their original coffers in a chapel specially built in Southover parish church.

Steyning parish church was built on the site of a demolished Saxon church by the monks of Fécamp. The chancel arch dates from *c*.1150 and the magnificent nave arcades and clerestory of some 50 years later are carved with a verve and detail which make them the best of their kind in Sussex. During the Tudor period the impoverished little town witnessed the demolition of the tower, crossing and choir. The present tower is a 16th-century structure built on to the west end of the nave.

The church of St Mary de Haura (of the Port) at Shoreham was built from 1103 by the de Braose family of Bramber Castle. Its size, before the collapse of most of the nave at some time in the 17th century, was larger than that of Southwark Cathedral and the sumptuousness of the choir, a masterpiece of 13th-century art, makes this one of the most extraordinary parish churches in England. The north and south arcade pillars differ in style; the former are late Norman and are attributed to masons from Canterbury Cathedral.

A number of downland churches, particularly Hardham, Coombes, Clayton and Plumpton, have medieval wall paintings which are the finest in England. They are usually attributed to *c.*1150 but may have been built earlier.

A Norman's home

Castle building was begun in earnest by the Normans. The plans of Pevensey, Hastings and Arundel, amongst the earliest castles, originally consisted of an earthwork mound (motte) with an attached fortified timber enclosure (bailey). From *c.*1150 these were replaced by great stone structures, repeatedly modified architecturally to take into account innovations in military weaponry and tactics. At Lewes a formidable shell keep was placed on a south-western mound. A further mound (Brack Mount), probably the site of the original castle, lies across the bailey to the north-east. A prominent barbican was erected in the 13th century and the castle substantially strengthened. Here the de Warennes, amongst the greatest of Norman magnates, resided in cramped and draughty quarters in rooms around a central courtyard. At Arundel the medieval stone keep on its mound, which replaced the wooden castle, and the 13th-century barbican survive. The rest of the castle was reduced to ruin in the Civil War and its present form is the creation of the Dukes of Norfolk from the end of the 18th century.

Top Places

◗ *1066 Country: Battle, Pevensey, Hastings*

◗ *Alciston barn and dovecote*

◗ *Crooked Ditch at Barnhorne, near Bexhill*

PORTS IN A STORM

THE TRADITION OF THE SEA

E ver since the open boats of the Bronze Age made for Shinewater
near Eastbourne, making a living from the sea, legally or other-
wise, was the main objective of Sussex people. They took
advantage of the narrows of the English Channel and of its being one of
the most crowded shipping lanes in the world. As seamen, fishermen,
shipbuilders, pirates and smugglers they brought fame or notoriety to
Sussex. Their symbols were the sailing cogs, luggers, ketches and hoys
that all slid by Sussex on the beam and entered or left its harbours whilst
engaged in the coastwise trade. They were followed later by the steam-
powered 'Sussex Coaster' which ended its days in the 1960s. But the
more adventurous crewed sturdy-hulled brigantines and three-masted
schooners, glorified trampships – working girls and proud of it – that
were built in Sussex shipyards and sailed through the Roaring Forties,
in the Southern Ocean, around the globe.

Despite wholesale rebuilding along the Sussex coast there is still
much visual evidence of past maritime history on every arm of the sea
– the sites of decaying quays, jetties, piers, old shipyards, warehouses
and fishing 'shops'. This draws attention to the sad decline in the coastal
trade and also to the vulnerability of the low and yielding shoreline to
the damaging effects of severe Channel storms at the moment of high
spring tides. Generally speaking, harbour-making in Sussex has been
difficult. Natural harbours were plentiful and the surge of high water

carried small sea-going vessels far inland, yet coastal processes over the centuries have trimmed back headlands sheltering harbours and silted them up with the resulting longshore drift of eroded material.

Man's constant struggles with these natural processes are an element in Sussex town-making. Sussex ports have tended to have a brief life-cycle: a short burst of activity, followed by early decline and a prolonged period of stagnation, when a new rival usurped its trade. Thus New Winchelsea succeeded Old Winchelsea before itself succumbing; New Shoreham was victorious over Old Shoreham and Steyning; Newhaven assumed the role of Seaford; and Littlehampton that of Arundel. Some ports met the final disaster of being drowned by the sea such as Pende, Cudlow and St Richard's, an outpost of Chichester.

Winchelsea

Old Winchelsea, which lay 3 miles (4.8 km) south-east of the present town, disappeared in the late 13th century, destroyed by decades of Channel storms, and was replaced by New Winchelsea founded by Edward I in 1288 on a hilltop promontory. To stand in its huge square and look up at the fragment of its noble church with its 'grand lines of arch and window' recalls the architectural glories of the age. A glance around at the chequerboard of streets is a reminder of the skills of 13th-century town planners and of the crucial importance of the port as a secure naval base in the French wars of the Kings Edward. Winchelsea was the most ambitious of the towns Edward I created, and was modelled on *bastides* (fortified towns in Gascony). The undertaking was never completed owing to attacks by the French, impoverishment from plagues and the silting up of the harbour. Nevertheless, Winchelsea has a significant place in the history of English town planning as one of the earliest towns laid out in a rectilinear pattern of streets.

Rye

The date of the origin of Rye is speculative. It has been plausibly suggested that the unnamed 'new borough' of 64 burgesses recorded in the Domesday Book can be identified with Rye. The extensive remains of its fortifications, including the massive Ypres Tower, the keep of the 13th-century castle, and the Land Gate, mark its important defensive role. As Winchelsea declined, so Rye reached its zenith and, strongly protected by its new walls, remained a powerful trading and fishing community into Elizabeth I's reign. By this time the retreat of the sea, aggravated by extensive 'inning' of the marshes (damming the tides with embankments), brought about a marked decline. Celia Fiennes, visiting in 1697, reported that the harbour was choked with sand. Rye is now a town of unparalleled ancient beauty and the whole hill over which its irregularly built streets and twittens, many still cobbled, and the close-piled, red-roofed houses spread, crowned by its noble parish church, takes on the character of a historic monument. It has an extraordinary atmosphere, more like the German and Dutch towns with which it was associated, than an English one. Its name is derived from Saxon *ie*, an island, and even up to the early 19th century the causeway connecting it to Winchelsea and London was perilous in stormy weather, as Turner captures in his brilliant watercolour of 1823.

Shoreham

Shoreham was another new town created in 1103, probably by William Braose I of Bramber Castle, to replace St Cuthman's port some 6 miles (9.7 km) upstream at Steyning and that of Old Shoreham, an episode which has left no traces apart from the beauty of the 11th-century church. Its ordered, rectilinear streets imply town planning and the splendid parish church standing in its own close was clearly intended to reflect honour on the town. The port's heyday was in the early Middle Ages when it was convenient for travel to and from the Angevin prop-erties of the English kings and for the embarkation of soldiers for the Crusades, numbers of which left crosses inscribed on the church pillars.

During the late 14th century the harbour began to silt up, appar-ently a consequence of the deflection of the shingle spit eastwards, and a series of disastrous storms destroyed much of the town. It is conceiv-able that the streets existing north of the High Street were replicated south of it, in which case half the town may have been lost. By the

16th century Shoreham fell into comparative obscurity and as late as 1801 it mustered less than 800 inhabitants. Its revival as a seaport and shipbuilding town was essentially due to the rise of Brighton. The harbour entrance was stabilised at its present position by an artificial cut through the shingle spit which had virtually strangled the town. The canalisation of an old course of the River Adur towards Brighton boosted trade still further and until the 1960s Shoreham was one of the most successful of the smaller English ports.

Seaford & Newhaven

On the River Ouse, Lewes was accessible to sea-going ships for centuries and until World War II barges reached the town. The present agricultural villages of Rodmell and Piddinghoe were engaged in the North Sea herring fishery at the time of Domesday. Despite the repeated raising of seawalls, the Ouse valley was devastated by late-14th century storms and the severe flood of 1421 which destroyed much of the Netherlands. The port on the estuary was Seaford which was associated with the Cinque Ports and handled the wool trade from the Ouse valley until the early 16th century when the new harbour was sited on the opposite side at Newhaven. Ever since, the town has been in a state of suspended animation, the low-lying open space in the centre of the town marking where its medieval wharves and warehouses once stood. The origin of Newhaven has been misunderstood. The traditional account is that the Ouse was diverted from Seaford to Newhaven by a violent storm in about 1565 but it has become apparent that the diversion of the Ouse was a deliberate act in about 1539 by local gentry to improve the navigation and drainage. This meant making a new cut directly to the sea at Newhaven, one of the earliest canalisations in England.

Top Places

❯ *Shoreham's little streets, parish church, and The Marlipins and its Museum*
❯ *The Fisherman's Museum on Brighton seafront*
❯ *The fishing 'shops' at Old Hastings*
❯ *Newhaven Museum*

MAKING THE DOWNS WORK

THE DOWNLANDERS

The Downs, as we have seen, are the oldest part of Sussex and one of the most anciently settled parts of England. Before the farming revolution from 1939 visitors had the intellectual shock of excitement at the illusion that the Downs had stood still and the past had taken over all its undulating landscape. Even now, walking the white tracks, we can physically stretch out and touch ancient earthworks, burial mounds, flint mines and remains of habitation several thousand years old. The silence of the present day, where once was so much life, makes it more penetrating and memorable.

The medieval scene

There is visual evidence, best seen in low winter light, of long curving strips rising from hillsides like a staircase. These lynchetted fieldstrips are not the short prehistoric or Romano-British type, but made by a big team of plough oxen. Examples are those visible from the road between Poynings and Edburton, above Lower Beeding, and on the flanks of Newtimber Hill.

This suggests a rise in population during the early Middle Ages which required the reclamation of marginal land. In the later Middle Ages the reverse occurred, a depletion of population leading to deserted and shrunken settlements and parish churches reduced in size –109 deserted settlements in Sussex, mainly on the Downs, have been identified.

The only site to have been excavated is Hangleton, near Brighton, now covered by a housing estate. In some cases a solitary church may suggest vanished homesteads as at Berwick, Beddingham, Hamsey and Warminghurst. At others a vanished chapel tells of decline, as at Balmer, Old Erringham, North Marden, Up Marden and Linch. A very common phenomenon is the shrunken village – Sullington, near Storrington is a good example. The Adur valley has three, Annington, Botolphs and Coombes; the Ouse valley has Tarring Neville and Sutton near Seaford; there is also Glyndebourne, Winton near Alfriston, and Alciston. The latter has 'lost' almost all the old houses which lined the street south of the Court Farm. With a trained eye an observer will note the present gappy nature of downland villages, spot the empty house platforms which are now merely allotments or gardens or spend time examining the humps and bumps which signify the desertion of a settlement.

Exploiting chalk

Diversifying the smooth chalk slopes are the small chalk quarries dotted on farmland all over the High Downs. Now abandoned, they are identifiable from afar by circular green hollows amidst an ocean of wheat and barley. They were dug for raw chalk which was applied to the leached red soils above the chalk to mellow and sweeten them when the land was brought into arable cultivation from the 18th century, and especially during the Napoleonic Wars and again from c.1860-80 when corn prices were high. The chalk was raised in buckets by a simple winch operated by a cart wheel. The raw chalk took over a year to dissolve but its effects were so long-lasting that soil analyses in the 1960s still indicated a beneficial effect.

The constant search for fertiliser and building material has left other vestiges of human action in the landscape. Old lime pits are common features, the most spectacular being on the banks of rivers where water transport was available to convey the lime into the Weald to ameliorate its acid soils. On the banks of the River Ouse, at and near Lewes, are more chalk quarries and workings than anywhere in Britain and Europe. There were also major quarries and lime works at Houghton, Amberley and Bury in West Sussex. Similar smaller works were sited all along the north-facing escarpment which is pock-marked by white hollows. Lime-kilns were ubiquitous. At the base of Duncton Hill is the unusually large one belonging to Lord Egremont of Petworth.

Dovecotes

Considerable numbers of dovecotes existed on the Downs when pigeons were raised for table during winter when fresh meat was scarce. At Charlton in West Sussex, a circular dovecote survives and at neighbouring West Dean there is a handsome square one. There is a double-chambered one in ruins at Alciston, near Lewes, once the property of the monks of Battle Abbey, a well-preserved round one at Firle and a beautifully restored one at Hangleton, near Brighton.

Working mills

Water mills were a familiar part of downland from Roman times. The largest of the 19th-century mills were the Bishopstone Tide Mills to which barges brought grain along the River Ouse. Sixteen grind stones were worked by the falling tide and over 100 people were employed there. The site is now well interpreted for the public. Duncton, near Petworth, is an example of a former watermill site converted to tourist use. Until comparatively recently the Downs would also have been dotted with windmills which were really beautiful, important and distinc-tive features. At least one and sometimes more were to be found in each parish or manor, but they disappeared rapidly with the coming of steam power. Halnaker Mill, famed in Hilaire Belloc's verses, is the only one still standing in that district. Polegate Tower Mill near Eastbourne has been restored and is in working order. Restored, but not operative, are the 'Jack and Jill' mills in Clayton and windmills at High Salvington near Worthing, West Blatchington near Hove, Oldlands at Keymer and the one at Rottingdean standing spectacularly dark on the steep turf ridge above the village. A number have been converted to living accommodation including Pipe Passage, Lewes, Patcham, Washington Rock, Alfriston and West Chiltington.

Gathering water

There is no visible water for miles around because the porosity of chalk means that excessive rain is absorbed through the pores of the rock instead of lying on the surface. One ubiquitous feature which overcame the lack of surface drainage was the dew pond. Constructed with great skill, this was a saucer-like depression dug out of the surface. The floor was covered with straw alternately with puddled clay. Two inches of burnt lime followed to prevent worms puncturing the clay and another layer of straw followed. Finally, a layer of rough earth was piled on top. This was thought to aid condensation of dew and mist, although actually the main source of water appears to have been rain. It is probable that the art of making them dates from prehistoric times. In recent years a number of dew ponds have been restored as habitats for great crested newts by The National Trust and the South Downs Society. Dried out dew ponds are marked by shallow depressions.

Villages had well-houses, such as that at East Marden which still exists. At Saddlescombe Farm, north of Brighton, a donkey wheel which drew water from a well 150 feet (46 metres) deep has been restored. A similar donkey wheel at Stanmer, near Brighton, raised water from a depth of 252 feet (77 metres).

Highways & bostals

The most distinctive highways are the droveways heading into the Weald. They are typically deeply worn into the face of the escarpment, but their oblique inclination enabled oxen and horses to drag heavy loads up and down them. Such trackways are known locally as 'bostals', a name probably derived from Saxon *beorg*, a hill, and *stig*, a path.

Farms & barns

The downland farmhouse is generally expressive of comfort and well-being and is often bigger than needed by the present owners. Larger ones, usually rebuilt in the late 18th or early 19th centuries are rather grand flint, stone or brick-built, some with the traditional Horsham slate roofs. A hall with a lofty ceiling, an elaborate candelabrum and grand fireplace would have been crammed with brass and pewterware and gilt-framed pictures would have crowded the wainscoted walls. In the roomy kitchen hams would have been hung and booted labourers would have had their meals there. The womenfolk would have run the dairy and the poultry.

The yard which, gently sloping downwards, was surrounded on all sides by buildings – great barns, cow-houses, ox-stalls and stables, open cart sheds for the ponderous wains, granaries, winnowing houses, lambing pens and lean-tos. A midden was heaped with manure for the garden and by a moss-grown wall was the pond.

Impressive features remaining are the massive barns of great age which stored the wool, hay and grain. Charlton Court near Steyning has a magnificent early 15th-century barn. The Firle estate has several great barns; John Ellman's barn at Glynde is also enormous, as is that at Bishopstone Manor Farm, once an estate of the bishops of Chichester, and Sullington Manor Farm near Storrington. Numerous 17th- and 18th-century examples exist. Remote barns on the High Downs are falling into dereliction. Some of the barns were built for 'cotting' sheep in bad weather and for lambing. A fine example is New Barn on an outlying part of Housedean Farm at Falmer. It comprised a hay barn for winter feed, two sheep pens with shelters and a stone-built shepherd's hut provided with a chimney.

At one time, every downland shepherd had a hut on the Downs in addition to his cottage on the farm. A simple cave excavated into the side of a bank was replaced with flint-built structures such as the shepherd's cot at Cornish Farm near Eastbourne. In turn this was succeeded by the mobile shed in which the shepherd kept his tools and medicine, some feed for his sheep, his own clothing and a bed used at lambing time.

Top Places

- Halnaker Mill, near Boxgrove
- Old Erringham deserted village and site of chapel (TQ206075)
- The Amberley Working Museum
- The Weald & Downland Museum

MAKING THE WEALD WORK

THE WOODLANDERS

The Weald is a region of marked individuality which has had an unusual history. Unlike the rest of Sussex and most of England, it remained a wilderness long after land had been brought into cultivation elsewhere. Its permanent colonisation did not begin until the clearance of woodland between *c*.1150 and *c*.1350. How was the wildwood destroyed? What did people live on while they were doing it? How many man-hours did it take to clear an acre? The author has had some thoughts on these matters but there is plenty of scope for further investigation.

It is clear that the making of the Weald was essentially the work of peasant farmers, for everything is small-scale and piecemeal. An interesting study can be made of a small part of the Weald to show how the landscape changed from the first phase of occupation, the pioneer stage, when migrants flowed in unceasingly, through the period of contracting population after the Black Death in 1350, the Tudor and Stuart revival and the boom in glass and iron industries, and the final demise of the peasant farmer. It is difficult for us today to imagine the fortitude and hardiness of generations of small farmers who battled stalwartly against an unforgiving soil and left a legacy of a man-made landscape of amazing beauty, unsurpassed in Europe.

For security and mutual support, farmers tended to live in clusters of three or four little farms on land they had cleared jointly. Latecomers, who had to share dwindling reserves of land, were known as 'assarters', and held smallholdings and cottages. Their minute fields can still be seen in some places, and the common name Assart is a clue to their former whereabouts.

Another form of settlement was the 'waste edge' straggle of cottages and smallholdings along the edges of commons and forests. When the population fell after the Black Death, the clusters of little farms tended to devolve into the single larger farms we are familiar with today, and in the Tudor and Stuart period there is evidence of more amalgamations of separately run farms into larger holdings.

Wealden woodcraft

Trees were not only the basis of the Wealden ecology but Wealdsmen were woodmen to the very core of their being. From the 13th century, woodcraft – coopering, basket-making, hurdle-making, wood-turning – was the essence of the Wealden economy. Its most distinctive form of tree farming was 'coppice with standards'. The standards – mainly oak, but also beech – went mainly for construction. The coppice, an understory of Spanish chestnut or hazel, was used as fuel for the glass and iron industries, for home-burning, and as the raw material for a vast range of wood products. Coppicing was done on a cyclical cutting programme of ten or more years depending on the species. Standards were thinned to about 12 to the acre and felled before they cast too much shade on the underwood. Oak timber for shipbuilding was more usually grown in hedgerows or parks so that trees could grow for longer, allowing them to produce large crowns with crooked boughs known as knees and elbows. All woodland was provided with earth banks to keep out cattle and deer, and a coppice would have a number of such banks because it was cut in parcels by rotation. When the new shoots were growing strongly from the cut stools the cattle were permitted to graze and browse. Although forestry has now sadly declined and conifers have been introduced, extensive areas of Sussex are still covered by coppice and standards and much of this is classified as ancient woodland, and therefore protected.

Hedges & shaws

The surviving chequer work of small hedged fields has been belatedly recognised as one of the chief glories of the English landscape. This is thanks to the pastoral practices of the small family farm, backbone of the Wealden economy for centuries. Dating the age of a Wealden hedge by eye is not so ridiculous as it sounds. For one thing, ancient hedge lines are not straight, but crooked, often S-shaped. This is the result of using a plough drawn by four or more oxen, which would need to be turned in, first leftwards and then round to the right when preparing for the difficult turn on the headland at the top of the field. Secondly, ancient hedges are invariably broad and run lavishly to many species of tree, shrub and woody plants, and harbour a multitude of wild flowers, small mammals and songbirds.

The naturalist Dr Max Hooper demonstrated that hedges tend to acquire additional species as they age. As a rule of thumb, he concluded that one additional species colonises a hedge every 100 years. So at one extreme is the skimpy hawthorn 'hedge' that defines most straight-sided modern enclosures, and at the other an ancient Wealden hedge which would contain eight or more species. Hooper's technique was to count in 30-yard (27-metre) lengths. This method has a wide margin of error if only because the pioneer farmer would have undoubtedly gathered several species of shrub to make his first hedge. Nevertheless, it is broadly true that Tudor and Stuart hedges on new enclosures contain fewer shrubs than earlier ones. Consequently, despite its obvious limitations, hedgerow dating is an instructive and entertaining way of understanding the shaping of the countryside. The surveys of ancient hedges so far completed have also stimulated the planting of new ones.

Shaws are also distinctive features of the Wealden landscape, especially in East Sussex. They are linear strips of woodland too wide to be called a hedge and typically lie in land too difficult to plough: alongside streams and at the edges of steep hillsides. Little research has been done on their origins and development. Many may have resulted from neglect or dereliction in bad times, or from the encroachment of trees onto the margins of fields which have not been cut back. Some could possibly be the surviving remains of woods planted when timber prices were high, and others planted for the preservation of game.

Timber-framed vernacular

The ancient vernacular architecture of the Weald was timber-framed buildings of oak with exposed timbers and infilling of lath and plaster. The standard house of relatively well-to-do families was of three bays (where a bay is the space between one principal post and the next). The majority of medieval houses have the roof ends hipped and a small open gabled section at the apex known as a gablet. By the later 14th century a larger and more luxuriant house style spread from Kent. It was known as the Wealden, and had an open hall of two bays; smoke from the fire eventually found its way out 'via the eyes of everyone in the room' through thatch or tile and the gablets at either end of the roof. Over time the roof timbers were stained with soot. From the 16th century a chimney was inserted and bedrooms built above the hall but soot remains as evidence of the former open hall. The typical family farm was a more modest affair with a limited range of wooden farm buildings. (Compare the downland farmhouse, *p.42*.)

Greenways & twiddly lanes

Apart from the droveways (*see p.42*) the Weald has an astonishing network of twiddly lanes, bridleways and footpaths, many of which were formerly unmetalled greenways used by horse riders. In the 18th century, when travel by carriage became more common, many greenways became obsolete. Today they are an important heritage, albeit inadequately studied and mapped.

Top Places

◎ *Fine hedges can be seen near Huggett's Furnace Farm, Mayfield, marking the boundary between the royal manor of Rotherfield and the Archbishop's manor of South Malling*

◎ *Traditional small-hedged landscape with crooked boundaries can be seen on the road from Burwash to Brightling*

◎ *Small greenways are still to be found in the parishes of Framfield and Buxted*

CHRISTIAN SUSSEX

CHURCHES, CHAPELS, ABBEYS & PRIORIES

Sussex has more than 200 interesting churches and it is one of the joys of exploring the county to discover them, although very few are as exceptionally fine as Boxgrove, Steyning, Shoreham and Winchelsea. Sussex has been a very conservative county and this finds expression in its pre-eminence for more pre-Conquest buildings, or parts of buildings, than in any other part of England.

Downland churches

The Saxon churches (*see p.27*) were succeeded by little, barn-like churches distinguished by their utter simplicity. They were built by local people from local materials, in effect by the people for the people, with their own sweat. Their modesty is due to the relative poverty and small population of the numerous downland communities. An obvious sign of a reduced population is the reduced scale of a number of churches, such as St Botolph's in the Adur valley which has lost its north aisle. Amongst the most moving of the downland churches are the Mardens in the emptiest Downs north of Chichester. North Marden is one of only four original single-cell apsidals in England.

Wealden churches

These have a different history. The earliest were probably wooden buildings in forest clearings until rebuilt in stone in the 12th and

13th centuries when colonists were pouring in to clear the woodland and settle on farms. They were then progressively enlarged to accommodate increasing congregations. Kirdford in West Sussex, for example, was almost doubled in size in the 13th century by the addition of a wide north aisle the whole length of nave and chancel. In the 14th century the chancel was extended and a sacristy built. All the building materials were local – Horsham stone for the roof, Bargate stone for the church walls and 'Sussex marble' for the fittings. It is a story repeated the Weald over. Since this was a region where craftsmen worked in wood, there are good specimens of the woodcarver's art in Wealden churches, as at Ticehurst which has a beautifully carved font cover that opens on hinges to reveal delicately wrought panels. Another prominent feature of Wealden churches is the great west towers, probably an influence from Kent where Tenterden has one of the earliest and most outstanding.

Non-conformist chapels

In the 18th century, the forest country and bordering towns such as Lewes were pulsating with fundamentalist religious sects. The Jirah Chapel in Lewes is a timber-framed building of 1805 built to spread the Calvinistic doctrines of the local coal-heaver William Huntingdon whose tomb is in the chapel. The Cade Street Chapel, near Heathfield, was erected in 1769 for the followers of George Gilbert, known as 'The Apostle of Sussex'. In 1905 a memorial was erected to the Protestant martyrs who were burnt at Lewes in the mid 16th century, and early 18th-century grave stones have terracotta relief plaques by Jonathan Harmer. There are several other Martyrs Memorials in the Sussex Weald.

The Roman Catholic survival

In West Sussex, Roman Catholicism centred on the families of the Duke of Norfolk at Arundel, the Northumberlands at Petworth, the Lumleys of Stansted, De La Warrs of Offington and the Montagues of Cowdray. Amongst the earliest recusants was the Caryll family who originated from the farmhouse called Benton's in Shipley. This and the Caryll properties of Lady Holt Park near Harting and West Grinstead Park near

Horsham, sheltered priests. The seventh John Caryll went into exile with James II. There is a portrait of him in the Priest's House at West Grinstead. The Catholic church adjoining was built in 1876 and on account of the long persistence of the faith there it has an exceptional place in the life of the Catholic Church in England.

The landscape historian finds ample interest in church monuments, particularly those which commemorate members of the great Sussex families of the past – the 40 Pelhams buried in Laughton Church, the dozen or more Shelleys of Michelgrove at Clapham, Montagues of Easebourne, Coverts of Slaugham, Jefferays of Chiddingly, Oxenbridges at Brede, Fullers of Brightling, Gages of Firle, Curteises of Wartling and Sackvilles at Withyham among them.

Victorian church restoration

This was often differently evaluated by contemporaries then than by 'expert opinion' today. At Patching, for example, Nairn in the Sussex volume of Pevsner's *Building of England* considers it 'bad' but a contemporary tablet placed by the piscine affectionately commends the lord of the manor, Sir Richard Hunter, for restoring it so beautifully.

The restoration of a number of Sussex churches by the Victorians aroused the wrath of William Morris's Society for the Protection of Ancient Buildings founded in 1877 and some of the language used was hardly Christian. His Society thought the tombs in Winchelsea Church were 'shamefully scraped' and wanted to bash the head of parson or architect against one of their gables. Philip Webb, Morris's deputy, considered Slaugham a lost cause after its 'sickly' restoration, was scathing about Worth, the 'witless fiddling at Burwash' and the 'damnation all touched' about Etchingham.

City churches

Paradoxically, Brighton, the city of pleasure was also the city of religious revival and is studded with magnificent churches. It is to the munificence of the family of the Rev. Henry Michell Wagner (d. 1870) that this is largely due. Before the Wagner churches, chapels of ease were built for fashionable people. H.M.Wagner built four churches for the use of all classes and on his death in 1870 St Martin's was built by his three sons in his memory. The eldest son, the Rev. Arthur Douglas Wagner built the church of the Annunciation and three other churches – SS Mary and Mary Magdalen (demolished 1963), St Bartholomew's and the Resurrection (since dismantled) from the proceeds of his father's will. St Bartholomew's, designed by Edmund Scott, is stunningly high and has a magnificent Arts and Crafts interior by Henry Wilson.

Monasteries

Other notable religious buildings arose in Sussex. Amongst the most representative were the Augustinian foundations established mainly in the 13th century at a time of renewed religious zeal at Hardham, near Pulborough, Hastings (later at Warbleton), Michelham, Pynham, Shulbrede and Tortington near Arundel. The Priory of Shulbrede was founded *c.*1200. Its chief feature is the fresco painting, the most celebrated of which represents animals on roughly painted green hills, drawing on the legend that animals become articulate on Christmas Day.

Easebourne Priory dates to the middle of the 13th century and stands at a gateway to the famous Tudor mansion of Cowdray. The refectory, now a community centre, forms a picturesque cluster of Tudor gables and chimneys. In 1444 the Bishop of Chichester suspended the flashy young prioress and ordered her to reduce her household and sell her furs to discharge the priory's debts. Dame Alicia Hill, the last prioress, who seems to have run a reformed nunnery, was the person who placed the curse of fire and water on the male children who perpetrated the eviction of herself and her nuns. The ruin of Tortington Priory was acquired by Sir Arthur Watts in 1996 who restored what remained of the north wall of the nave into a thatched barn so sensitively that it won architectural awards.

Top Places

◗ Hardham, for the murals in the church and site of the Priory

◗ Coombes Church in the Adur valley and Didling near Pulborough, simple downland churches

◗ The site of Lewes Priory

COMMERCE & CASTLES

OLD MARKET & COUNTY TOWNS

LEWES is a rare gem, in many ways a quintessential English country town, small, compact and relatively unspoiled, complete with its ruined castle, its surviving coaching inn, some fine townhouses and still largely 'uncloned' shops, though now without its market. It seems to fulfil all the needs of a town at exactly the right size for a distinctive community in which everyone seems to know everyone else.

William Morris at the end of the 19th century thought Lewes looked like a box of toys from the brow of the hill above Falmer but it is now in danger of being enlarged out of recognition. The town piled high about its castle and its break-neck streets and tangle of little alleys, 'twittens', and the remains of its walls are reminders of its origin as a fortified town. The Downs surround it, their invigorating breezes pervade it, and there is the smell of the sea to recall that it was once a seaport.

Lewes is full of historic buildings. Southover High Street alone is crowded with interest. Anne of Cleves House is an early 16th-century Wealden hall house which is now a museum of local history. The gabled Bull House by the site of the Westgate was a medieval inn before becoming a townhouse belonging to the Goring family in the 16th century and being partially converted into the Westgate Chapel in 1700. It was subsequently the home of Thomas Paine, the local exciseman and revolutionary who lived in the town between 1768-74. He was a member of the Headstrong Club, a debating society that met at the

White Hart, which re-fronted in the early 19th century, has timbered ceilings inside. One of the joys of Lewes is the beauty of its flint buildings at the western entrance to the town.

Chichester

Founded by the Romans, the main outline of the streets is essentially theirs and the circuit of the city walls is almost perfect. It has little urban sprawl and many of the large gardens and orchards that lay behind the street frontages still exist. It retains old hospitals and schools, some of the little town churches, and the Butter Cross, the 16th-century market cross at the junction of the four streets. The north-east quadrant has a special character as the site of the Bishop's Palace, the Deanery, the houses of the canons and lesser cathedral clergy and the medieval Vicar's Hall which inspired Keats to write The Eve of St Agnes. Not far off is the mound on which the castle stood.

What also makes Chichester so exciting is its Georgian character. Much of its architecture is outstandingly good and gracious buildings survive not singly or in small groups but in whole quarters. Thomas Sharp, the post-war town planner, regarded Chichester as the least spoiled example in England of a naturally evolved Georgian town, as distinct from a deliberately planned one like Bath, and it was John Betjeman's favourite cathedral city. The Pallants is an exceptionally good Georgian quarter of former merchants' houses which now includes the Pallant Art Gallery. The Georgian character of Chichester bespeaks its prosperity as a market town in the centre of the great wheat-producing district. With the intensification of agriculture the Chichester Canal was completed in 1823 to connect to Portsmouth and the Arun and Wey Canal. Its short-lived existence is marked by a number of old buildings at the Canal Basin.

Chichester Cathedral has not the grandeur of Chartres, its sister city, nor such a magnificent collection of stained glass and sculpture. As Ian Nairn remarked in the Sussex volume of the *Buildings of England* series, 'it is a comfortable fireside chair cathedral'. Nevertheless the slim spire is the focal point of the exquisite view of the sea, the Isle of Wight and the Downs from the Trundle, Kingley Vale or Gumber Corner.

Steyning

Steyning is another good example of an old market town. Hadrian Allcroft in Downland Pathways (1924) thought he had failed to find a more pleasant town, 'the little place is just what one dreams of and its own surrounding require, neither too big nor too small, neither too formal nor too formless, neither too old nor altogether new, a perfect blend of all things desirable'. The same could be said today. The High Street alone is worth a long visit for its red-hot pantiles, dark slates and Horsham stone and the elaborate barge boards to the gables. Church Street has the famous Grammar School and the splendid 11th-century parish church, perhaps the very best in Sussex. Frank Duke and Ernest Cox made a valiant attempt to survey the houses in 1954, and the resulting book is probably unique in being a record of every individual house, each with its associations. More recently, the husband and wife team, H.M. and V.E. Lacey, have discovered numerous half-timbered buildings disguised under Georgian facades or shop fronts.

Horsham

Horsham was described in 1965 by Ian Nairn as 'an exasperating, traffic-laden, half-realized town' which despite being the main centre for the western Weald for centuries, with the Assize and Quarter Sessions, had never acquired impressive buildings or a real urban air. This is no longer true today for after a massive redevelopment the town has a go-ahead image. The best attributes remain, e.g. the delightful Causeway, the great church of St Mary with its magnificent, oak-shingled, broached spire and memorials to the Braose and Shelley families.

Arundel

Arundel is a town that has gripped the imagination for more than 200 years. John Martin Robinson has written of the ravishing beauty of the red-roofed hillside town crowned by a huge French Gothic cathedral and still more huge castle and of the improbable vision that greets the traveller by train which combines Conway, Amiens and Claude Lorrain. The town began around the motte-and-bailey castle erected by Earl Roger of Montgomery soon after the Conquest. The medieval keep on its mound and the 13th-century barbican survive but the castle was reduced to ruin in the Civil War and in its present form it is a creation of the Dukes of Norfolk from the 18th century. Arundel's parish church of St Nicholas unusually houses both the Anglican and Catholic denominations, divided by a glass screen. The steep side streets falling to the Arun have rows of cottages and larger houses, some open during the town's annual arts festival at the end of August.

Petworth

Petworth is still overshadowed by its feudal past and by Petworth House, once the home of the proud Percys, the even prouder Seymours and also the most extraordinary of its owners, the third Earl of Egremont (1751-1837). Almost the whole population of Petworth was once dependent on the owners of the great house for employment and so vast was the extent of the Petworth estate that the perimeter wall extends for some 16 miles (25.7 km). The fine landscaped park has been described by Marcus Binney as 'one of the most magnificent and best preserved and extensive of "Capability" Brown landscapes in England'. The gardens are associated with Fred Streeter, the national broadcaster, head gardener there from 1929 to 1969. The town huddles closely against the lofty walls of the house and forms one of the finest groups of domestic architecture in Britain.

Battle

Battle was a new town which grew outside the Abbey founded by William the Conqueror as a thanksgiving for his victory in 1066. He also granted a banlieu, or 'leuga', a roughly circular estate 3 miles (4.8 km) in diameter for its maintenance. This seems to have been virtually uninhabited but through the Abbey settlers and resources quickly flowed in. By 1110 a town of 109 households had arisen and this expanded further during the Middle Ages. The present town is a medley of houses and shops with a parish church containing the restored tomb of Sir Anthony Browne and his wife, inheritors of the Abbey at the Dissolution.

Top Places

❍ *Also worth a visit: Midhurst, for timber-framed buildings, brick fronts and estate cottages*

❍ *Also worth a visit: East Grinstead for Sackville Collge and St Margaret's Convent*

WORKING THE LAND

TUDOR & STUART HEAVY INDUSTRY

Sussex was the foremost centre for iron manufacture during most of the Roman occupation and in the 17th and 18th centuries, and was a major venue for glass-making in Elizabethan times. It also had a flourishing woollen industry in the Petworth district and on the Kentish border until it was transferred to the coalfields from the 18th century. The use of clay for pottery and bricks has also had a long history.

The landscape of ironmaking

Only the timid will be put off by the fact that, remarkably, the iron industry has left few obvious traces of its existence, for a careful, if arduous, search in woodland will often reveal a spot where an iron furnace or forge was worked. Even so, a great effort of imagination is required to visualise the scores of men coppicing timber for fuel, digging and roasting the ore, making pig-iron in the furnace and hammering iron into shape at the forge, and the clatter of the mill wheels, the thump-thump of the hammers and the smoke and flames. Usually the masonry of furnace or forge has been demolished and reused locally, and the wooden water wheel driving the bellows has decayed. Slag from a blast furnace is a black glassy substance and this is traceable in the banks of nearby streams or scattered around. The cinder from a forge forms waste heaps. The most impressive evidence is an earthen dam (a 'bay' in ironmaster's jargon) built across a stream to provide a head of water to power the bellows of furnace or forge. This will normally be concealed by trees and shrubs. To trace the drained-out millpond behind normally means observing carefully a meadow with clearly marked sides. Further downstream would have been a chain of long, narrow ponds ('hammer ponds'), providing a reservoir of water in summer when streams ran dry.

The iron ore was extracted by means of bell-pits, called 'Mine Pits'. Typically ore was found about 20-30 feet (6-9 metres) above the junction of the Wadhurst Clay with the Ashdown Beds. A surviving site is usually in woodland because the pits were filled in on land used for farming, often revealed by a series of shallow depressions which hold water after heavy rain.

Apart from Hendall Manor, near Heron's Ghyll, ironmasters' houses deserve a hunt. Gravetye, near East Grinstead (now a Country House Hotel), was built for Richard Infield and his wife Katherine. It is one of the loveliest 17th-century houses. Walter Burrell lived at Ockenden Manor in Cuckfield, also now a Country House Hotel. The Coverts of the now largely ruined Slaugham Place added iron to their activities. Field names, taken from current OS maps and tithe maps of the parish in County Record Offices in Lewes and Chichester, will help pinpoint sites, e.g. Hammer, Furnace Wood, Mine Pit Shaw.

The glass industry

This appears to have begun around Chiddingfold and Kirdford on the Surrey-Sussex border in the 13th century and spread in the 16th century to Wisborough Green, then the main centre, and to neighbouring parishes. Sand lenses in the Weald Clay were the basic material. Beech was preferred for its greater heat and pollarded trees are still characteristic of the area, together with a heavily wooded district which produced the prodigious quantities of fuel needed. This can be seen at Idehurst, the home of the glass-making Strudwick family, and one of the most fascinating of the old houses in the Low Weald near Kirdford. Some 42 glass-making sites have been identified but the stone used in construction of glasshouses has been robbed and there is little evidence on the ground.

The cloth industry

Outworkers wove cloth in their cottage homes in the vicinity of Midhurst, Petworth, Lodsworth, Arundel, Chichester, Kirdford and Steyning and sent it to their nearest town or village for dyeing and finishing. Similarly Buxted, Framfield, Frant and Robertsbridge were outliers of Cranbrook in Kent, the principal cloth centre in south-east England.

The most obvious visual signs of prosperous cloth-making in the past are unusually large and well-built yeomen's houses in the village street. They are often distinguished by comparatively large first-floor windows, which lighted the loom, or wide overhanging upper rooms which provide extra space for weaving. The delightful village of Lodsworth has such houses and some of the larger and more dignified houses in Petworth, Midhurst and Steyning are also owed to the cloth trade.

Brick-making

Bricks were reintroduced into Sussex in the 15th century, taking advantage of the ample supplies of clay, sand and fuel. Bricks were normally made in small-scale kilns on commons. Herstmonceux Castle, built in the 1440s was the first brick-built building in Sussex. The Dacre family who built the castle added their chapel to the parish church in brick. East Guldeford church near Rye was built in brick in the 1490s and Twineham church in the 1520s. In the 16th century, brickyards and tileries began to multiply, as at Battle and Alciston, but only the wealthy were able to build in brick. The tower of the former home of the Tudor Pelhams (now owned by the Landmark Trust), Danny at Hurstpierpoint, Cuckfield Place and Leigh Manor in Cuckfield, Halland near East Hoathly are amongst the finest surviving examples of 16th-century brickwork.

Top Places

- ❯ *Hammer ponds south of Horsham and those in Leonardslee*
- ❯ *Mine Pit Shaw in Burwash*
- ❯ *Burwash Forge, reached by a greenway through woodland from Kipling's mill at Batemans*
- ❯ *Hendall Manor near Heron's Ghyll*
- ❯ *Lodsworth village for its fine clothiers' cottages*
- ❯ *Kirdford Church, to see the recently added stained glass windows created from 16th- and 17th-century 'green' glass made locally by French entrepreneurs*

FIRST RESORTS

SUSSEX BY THE SEA

The Sussex coast was greatly modified by the social movement of sea-bathing for health which became fashionable amongst the wealthy in the second half of the 18th century. As Jane Austen implied in her unfinished fragment *Sanditon* (1817), fledgling seaside resorts marketed by speculative adventurers sprang up as if by magic and followed in the wake of Hastings and Brighton, engulfing with remarkable rapidity long stretches of the 70-mile (113-km) coastline with little microcosms of London. The elite found the impetus irresistible. The fishing town of Brighton became the very acme of the English bathing resort and in presenting 'mile after mile, its gay and fantastic front to the sea', entered on a new lease of life. By 1843 A.L. Wigan reported in his *Brighton and its Three Climates* that it had become the 'great sanitarium [of] the largest and wealthiest city in the world'. It seemed to many observers that eventually 'every paltry village on the Sussex coast which had a convenient beach will rise to a considerable town'. This prophecy can be said to have been realised during the inter-war years.

The birth of the seaside

The development of a Sussex sea-bathing resort tended to fall into distinct stages, each with its own imprint on the present scene. In the embryonic stage of growth, speculators raised rows of lodgings facing away from the sea, wherever there was a suitable beach and level ground.

The houses were intended for seasonal letting to the nobility and gentry and were normally tall, narrow terraced houses, four or five storeys high with low bow windows to take advantage of the sun and provide a view of the social scene below. The interiors were generally very plain. Libraries, assembly rooms, a promenade, and the other recreational facilities were provided in imitation of Bath and other inland spas. All these amenities were laid out without any conscious plan.

The next stage of growth was marked by the erection of terraces, squares and crescents as single architectural compositions by one architect or landlord, again in the manner of Bath. The majority fronted the sea and contained graceful, well proportioned buildings, reflecting the more successful resorts' rising taste and greater assurance. Brighton attained this stage in 1798; Hastings and Worthing did not reach it until 20 years later; Eastbourne's growth was arrested at the first stage for half a century; Seaford never evolved from the first stage at all. Lancing did even worse: an enterprising proprietor advertised bathing machines but even 20 years later he had built only a single lodging.

A further stage is marked by the more comprehensive development represented by the systematic planning of large estates on virgin ground to create integrated communities in the style of Nash's Regent's Park development. Brighton and Hastings entered this phase in the 1820s, but Worthing, Littlehampton and Bognor achieved little in this respect.

The new resorts

BRIGHTON: few places have entered so far into the public consciousness and few have offered such an astonishing variety of experiences. It was wrong of early Brightonians to boast that the city had arisen from a fishing village. In fact it was a large fishing town, though not very prosperous, before it became a resort. It has also been proved that Dr Richard Russell did not 'invent' Brighton when he published his influential book on the use of sea water in curing glandular diseases. He evidently came to Brighton in 1753 because already the resort was stirring. Brighton enjoyed the three essential conditions for a resort's success – accessibility to London, approval of the medical profession and royal patronage.

As London's nearest point on the south coast it had an immense advantage over its rivals; a few miles made more difference then than it does today. By the 1820s the fastest coaches covered the 51 miles (82 km) from the capital in five hours. Brighton was also fortunate in having a long line of articulate physicians who extolled the properties of its sea air. Above all, Brighton owed most to its presiding genius, the Prince Regent, who hardly missed a season's residence there between 1783 and 1826.

The Old Town of Brighton has a special character of its own which still has a continuity with the community which lived by fishing. Now known as 'The Lanes' it is the tangle of alleys in a cramped, compact layout which Charles II knew when he was propelled to France. This contrasts with the ordered unity of building design of c.1780-1800 around the Steine where fishermen originally drew up their boats and dried their nets, and the sustained development that followed. The set-piece was the Royal Pavilion itself, and the processional magnificence of classically designed buildings along the sea front, hitherto unexploited. This reflects the self-assurance of a town which had outstripped its rivals.

HASTINGS developed slowly. Even in 1804 the town had only two streets, High Street and All Saints, and its library dates only from 1788. Its real prosperity was deferred until the early 19th century when under the influence of the Romantic Movement its delightful cliffs, coves and wooded scenery, as well as the mildness of its air were appreciated. It equipped itself with an esplanade in 1812 and a pier in 1872.

Its growing popularity induced James Burton, a great London builder, who designed part of Regent's Park, to purchase land on which to build.

ST LEONARDS was created from scratch in 1828. It had an elegant sense of design lacking in Hastings which attracted fashionables who particularly enjoyed the mildness of the Marina in winter compared with Brighton's exposure. Only the crescents of Bath and Brighton rival the Italianate villas on the hillside overlooking the town.

BOGNOR was a small fishing village until 1785 when Sir Richard Hotham, 'the London hatter' as Dr Johnson scornfully called him, began to build lodgings, making it the earliest seaside resort to be promoted by one man. It became known as a 'quiet watering-place' for those desiring seclusion with the same luxury and refinement as at Brighton. His showpiece was Hothampton Crescent (now part of the University of Chichester). Its central residence, the Dome, has been described as 'the best example of 18th-century work at any seaside town in Sussex'. Although much booming was done after Hotham's death, Worthing gained an ascendancy over it and little building took place after the 1820s until the modern period.

WORTHING began with rapid growth in the late 18th century and then suffered a long period of arrested development from the 1820s, leaving it for several decades with sporadically dispersed buildings amongst farmland. It still exemplifies an extreme form of the amorphous town plan of early resorts with no recognisable focus. It was consciously designed as a cheaper and quieter version of Brighton. By 1812, boosted by Princess Amelia's stay in the town and other royal patronage, it was a complete resort and its progress seemed assured. It suffered, however, from a fall in visitors after the end of the Napoleonic Wars and the deadly blow of losing the universal approval of the medical profession, apparently due to inadequate sanitation. The most notable buildings erected in the 1820s and 1830s were the colonnaded Liverpool Place and Park Crescent. A good example of the lack of an overall plan is that a row of delightfully balconied houses originally fronting the sea was later hidden by a mid-Victorian building.

EASTBOURNE started early as a resort but remained in the shadows until the 1860s on account, it was said, of the reluctance of the largest landowners, the Cavendishes, to change the character of their country retreat of Compton Place. The reversal of this policy began from 1858 when the seventh Duke of Devonshire inherited the estate. He committed a large part of his fortune in an ecstasy of building of such taste and quality that Eastbourne became known as the 'Empress of Watering Places' in the 1889s. The town was conceived in the grandest manner and, intentionally or not, outrivalled all but the very best of Brighton. Contrastingly, the development on the other large estate, that of the Gilberts, is composed of medium-sized and small villas.

HOVE, once a little fishing village, was separated from Brunswick Town by a mile of farmland until the 1850s. Its separate identity as a residential town rather than a resort is due to two generations of building in the second half of the 19th century. To walk the streets of Hove today is to pass successively through the sequence of architectural styles which rapidly followed one another at the time. Goldsmid's Adelaide Square, in the manner of Bayswater or Belgravia, was the last of the classical. A complete break with the past was Gallard's Cliftonville with its well-to-do villas. Then came the Stanford Estate, owned by Thomas Stanford, lord of the manor of Preston, on its own tract of undeveloped land. This was intended as a showpiece of dignity and opulence based on a rectilinear pattern of spacious avenues, the widest not named but numbered in the manner of American boulevards. Piecemeal development over some 40 years inevitably caused some stylistic chaos and it is organically unrelated to the rest of Hove. Henry Earp senior's painting of the unspoiled downland village of Portslade in 1840 also just caught the scene before it was similarly covered in buildings.

BEXHILL in its modern guise is largely the creation of the seventh Earl De La Warr who began to develop it when the income from his agricultural estate began to decline. From the beginning his intention was to create a resort of high-quality housing, hotels and entertainment. From 1892 his son continued the project and was notable for the new sport of motor racing which he brought to Bexhill in 1902, as well as international cycling tournaments. His progressive views led to the town being the first in the country to permit mixed bathing. The ninth Earl (d. 1976) sponsored the modernist De La Warr Pavilion in 1935, an iconic building on the south coast and acclaimed internationally.

Top Places

◗ *De La Warr Pavilion, Bexhill*
◗ *The Royal Pavilion, Brighton*
◗ *The First to Fourth and Grand Avenue, Hove*
◗ *The monument to the seventh Duke of Devonshire and its surrounds at Eastbourne*

THE COUNTRY HOUSE

GARDENS, PARKS & ESTATES

O ne of the most distinctive characteristics of much of Sussex is the type of landscape designed to combine business with leisure and pleasure. H.G. Wells, who was very familiar with Uppark House, thought that in Sussex this had been elevated above anywhere else in Britain. First there were deer parks and forests set aside for hunting. Then came the country house set in a park (generally a former deer park) by the established aristocracy and gentry. These in turn were taken over by stockbrokers and City people and those who had made their profits from the coalfields or overseas. Newly created ones also multiplied in the period of agricultural decline between the 1870s and World War II. Then mostly they disappeared, and their estates were broken up, in a holocaust which foreigners might have thought could only have been the work of communist revolutionaries.

The country house landscape

The country house has had a remarkable effect on the Sussex landscape. Christopher Hussey (1899-1970), quondam editor of *Country Life*, who himself came to own Scotney Castle remarked that the various kinds of its landscaping activity to 'reshape' woods, downs and fields on many estates into 'a vast, newly created landscape natural enough to our eyes, but in reality managed as much for picturesque appearances as for economic returns'. What Hussey meant was that many country house owners had turned the whole of their estate into a kind of garden by extending landscaping in lessening degrees beyond the garden and park out to the home farm, the tenant farms and the boundaries of the estate. This had been advocated by Joseph Addison in the early 18th century and was favoured at that time by Alexander Pope and Stephen Switzer.

In the mid-19th century the landscaping advocate was J.C. Loudon in his *Encylopadedia of Cottage, Farm and Villa Architecture* (1842). Apart from the terrace, garden and park, he envisaged concealing prosaic buildings in trees, erecting eye-catchers here and there to be seen from the windows of the house, erecting a model farmery and model cottages for tenants, interspersing copses for beauty and game preservation, lavishly planting up hedgerows and concealing the boundaries of the estate by belts of trees. He wanted the whole estate to have a unity created by a powerful design which interwove the various components into a single, all-embracing composition designed to unfold before the eye, not as a collection of unrelated parts but as a flowing succession of harmonised pictures.

The pleasure farm

At a lower level of activity was the 'pleasure farm', a toy estate. This developed in late Victorian and Edwardian times from the 18th-century *ferme ornée* (ornamental or villa farm). The traveller bowling along the newly turnpiked Brighton Road in the 1830s had the agreeable sight of a succession of artistically designed 'cottages' in grounds laid out for the two objectives of beauty and usefulness. On the little estate, rides were opened up in woodland to give prospects of neat tenant cottages, and livestock implausibly gave an impression of agriculture. The repair of old hedges was advised as was a free planting of trees and the planting up of the headlands of fields turned over to pasture. The pleasure farm also imparted a widespread park-like appearance to farmland. It was typically found in the Weald on the outskirts of Brighton and around the growing towns of the 'London sort' like Haywards Heath. Typically, a former farmhouse would be enlarged and trees on the margins of fields thickened into shaws (belts of timber between fields), straight lines rounded off and the landscape beautified in various ways in everyone's eyes except the farming fraternity and others like John Halsham, who steadfastly held to the 'old' Sussex and did not value land as a playground and a place where people could wander at will and admire the scenery.

The end of landscaping

Much of this landscaping has been destroyed through neglect or destruction since the depression in the 1930s and the exigencies of the circumstances since the last war. Even shortly after World War I the country house already belonged to the past. Taxation and death duties, first imposed by Lloyd George in his 1909 Budget, made the occupation of country houses virtually impossible and to survive they were put to new uses such as hospitals, schools, mental homes and other institutions. When World War II arrived they were requisitioned by the armed forces and government departments while the family either departed or retired disconsolately to the wings. After the war owners admitted paying visitors, or put their properties up for sale, and many country houses fell into the hands of the National Trust. Meanwhile much of the rich beauty of the landscape diminished, though it survives triumphantly on such estates as Goodwood, Cowdray and Arundel.

'Lost' country houses

Country houses which have been demolished or put to new uses might be called 'lost'. In Sussex there are several hundred but the actual figure is uncalculated at present. John Harris, the architectural historian, visited a number of these 'lost' houses and recounts his experiences in *No Voices From The Hall* (1998). When he visited Slindon House, now a school – formerly a palace of the Archbishops of Canterbury and afterwards the home of the Isaacsons who donated it and almost the whole village to the National Trust – he found the brooding silence of empty rooms and a locked range of cupboards packed with precious porcelain wrapped in newspapers, the fate of which remains a mystery. At West Grinstead Park, a castellated villa designed by John Nash for Walter Burrell in 1806, the once fine circular living room was being used for the storage of potatoes.

The most magnificent is Cowdray, a Tudor house succeeding the fortified manor house of the Bohuns, which is traceable as foundations on nearby St Ann's Hill in Midhurst, and is of spectacular interest not only architecturally but because it was associated with the heart of Tudor government. In 1793, only days before the drowning of the eighth Viscount Montague, the descendant of Sir Anthony Browne, the first owner, the magnificent house was almost completely destroyed by fire. These happenings were said to have fulfilled a prophecy of the last Prioress of Easebourne (*see p.51*) who put a curse of fire and water on the house when the nuns were turned out. Fortunately, the Swiss artist Hieronymus Grimm has made drawings at Cowdray (including the paintings it contained) before the fire and Richard Gough made notes in the 18th century which have enabled a reconstruction to be made. The eastern range of the house is comparatively complete as is the three-storey Gate House. The Great Hall with its mullioned windows together with the Great Staircase and other once splendid rooms can be made out.

Another Tudor mansion now in ruins is Slaugham Place, near Handcross, designed by James Thorpe, the architect of Longleat in Wiltshire. The kitchen ovens and fragments of the hall and undercroft remain together with a dramatic loggia of three surviving arches. The fine terrace and the Tudor lodges at the corners of the garden walls contribute to the Elizabethan atmosphere.

Ashdown House, a large country house standing in its own park near Forest Row was designed in 1793 by the young Benjamin Latrobe (1764-1820) who emigrated to America and was responsible for the cathedral at Baltimore and the Capitol in Washington. In 1792 he had designed neighbouring Hammerwood House, Doric and masculine in design (and miraculously saved by the Pinnegar family in 1982), whereas Ashdown House is Ionic and feminine in style. The inspiration for its circular portico and entrance hall were drawn from Periclean Athens.

Top Places

- ◉ *Knepp Castle Estate, Shipley, near Horsham, an estate being 'wilded'*
- ◉ *The Goodwood Estate near Chichester*
- ◉ *Scotney Castle, Lamberhurst, a splendid example of the Picturesque*

NATURE ENHANCED
GREAT LANDSCAPE GARDENS

Sussex has been perceived for centuries as a refuge of peace from the stressful world outside. Consequently it is one of those parts of England where almost all the wealthy went a'gardening, that most restful and meditative of activities. The established aristocracy and gentry were passionately fond of gardening and rectors followed suit, together with retired service officers and professional people. The *nouveau riches* poured in from the late 19th century with their profits from the City, the coalfields or overseas, and cottagers caught the bug from their betters. The fact that much of Sussex became marginal to agriculture following the imports of grain and meat with Free Trade from the 1870s meant that farmland went cheap to newcomers and the heavy moisture content of Wealden soils made them most apt for the growth of trees and shrubs. The 18th-century landscape designer Humphry Repton summed this up succinctly when he remarked of Sheffield Park that in Sussex, 'every berry became a bush and every bush a tree' and said of his art in relationship to the Sussex scene 'that it is only a question of whether you do not spoil Nature's work'.

Landscape genius

Before William Robinson, the Victorian gardener and writer, Sussex gardens had been imitations of those in Italy and France. Their creators had seen them through the eyes of Claude and Poussin and attempted to reproduce in English scenery the artists' transcripts of the landscape around Rome and Tivoli. The age of achievement in English park landscaping had ended by 1830. This led to the wish for a new inspiration. Forestry began to be considered as a reservoir for hardy plants brought back by collectors from cool and temperate parts of the world.

The best artistic medium for these purposes proved to be the 'wild' or woodland and other natural gardens popularised from the 1870s by Robinson. The essence of his principle was that hardy plants both thrived and looked better if planted in the natural manner of their wild habitats. Robinson drew his inspiration directly from the 'genius' of the landscape itself, the semi-vestigial historic wildness of the Weald, which still survived enough to encourage the fancy for 'wildness'.

His uncommon gifts and exceptional energy touched every aspect of the arrangement and management of bold natural groups of plants and trees. His *Alpine Flowers For English Gardens* (1870) was a corrective to the general view that alpines could not be successfully grown in England. This caught the public fancy at a time when enthusiasm was growing for Swiss mountaineering and travel. Gardeners began to introduce in miniature something of the effects of mountain scenery by making use of rocky outcrops and deep natural ravines (called 'ghylls' in the Weald), and by constructing rockeries from locally quarried sandstone. Many old mill streams, marl and mine pits and disused hammer ponds were transformed into 'wild' gardens under the stimulus of Robinson's *Wild Garden* (1870), which encouraged the naturalising of early bulbs in meadows, around dull shrubberies, among underwood and in hedgerows. Nearer the house, Robinson re-established the herbaceous border for the Victorian bedding-out of geraniums.

William Robinson's garden at Gravetye Manor near East Grinstead is the setting for an Elizabethan mansion of broad mullioned windows and tall dormers built for Richard Infield, an ironmaster, and his wife Katherine in 1598 (*see p. 57*). Robinson bought a number of small, semi-derelict farms and took the unfashionable decision not to turn the fields into a park. He thought that the traditional chequer work of little hedged fields was the prettier landscape.

In preparation for his landscaping, Robinson adapted everything on his estate – 'every field, every wood, every cottage, every farmhouse, every road and every fence had to be overhauled... Everything was done with regard to landscape beauty, whether roadside fence, plantation, covert, all was done with that in view'. In his book *Gravetye Manor* (1911) Robinson recorded each year's work in the grounds. Uniquely, one can visualise through his diary the gradual evolution of one of the world's outstanding gardens. The whole of his new estate was embraced in his plans and as a tree planter Robinson has no peer but John Evelyn.

Great gardens

Enjoying these gardens today one can still sense the excitement with which Sussex landowners discussed and exchanged newly discovered seed from the temperate regions of the Himalayas and the Caucasus, western and central China, Japan, Tasmania and New Zealand that they had either collected on challenging expeditions of their own or acquired through sponsoring such collectors as Frank Kingdon-Ward and George Forrest. Robinson's garden expressed the mood of the age and his own work at Gravetye and his books were partially responsible for the rapid spread of wild gardens in the Weald. Colonel Stephenson Clarke, who also began to plant at Borde Hill near Haywards Heath in the 1890s, placed on record his first efforts in shutting out unsightly views and improving the landscape generally on the whole of his estate. He went on to plant hardy trees and shrubs on an extensive scale on the principles expounded by Robinson.

Another who greatly changed the appearance of his estate was the late Victorian poet and writer Coventry Patmore (1823-96) who described his joy when working with axe and saw at Heron's Ghyll on the edge of Ashdown Forest and 'releasing into the blue distance' prospects which had long been shut in by dense trees. He also recorded his scheme for planting, draining and damming for lakes.

Leonard Messel's garden, Nymans at Handcross, is also important in the history of gardening. He thought nothing of travelling to New Zealand for exotic species. It was a common practice at the end of the

19th century to start exotic plants in heated houses. They failed so often that Messel tried the experiment of bringing on seedlings in an old sheltered paddock. These proved stronger and hardier when planted out. He created an excellent heath garden.

Leonardslee, the famous garden planted by Sir Edmund Loder in the 1890s is an inspiring situation of enchanting loveliness. It is the perfect wild garden with infinitely diversified landscapes of wooded hillsides, long winding paths, lily-margined lakes and running streams in which plants and trees imported from America, Asia, Africa and Australia have been acclimatised without losing the native woodland character of the setting. Especially famous were Loder's scented strains of Loderi rhodo-dendron hybrids, planted in quantity. The great storm of October 1987 proved a blessing. Robin Loder explained that trees had been planted too thickly to appreciate fully the beauty of the setting and parts were too gloomy. The storm blew away the gloom and saved the garden.

South Lodge, Lower Beeding, was the creation of the Godman family in the late 19th century. Their 'wild' or woodland garden marks a new stage in the appreciation of nature by owners who had a flair for land-scape gardening and who were artists and naturalists in outlook.

F.C. Stern's Chalk Garden on the flanks of Highdown Hill above Worthing is famed for the success he had with planting on virgin chalk from 1909. He found that, provided the thin chalk soil was well cultivated and mulched, plants that had no dislike of lime would flourish. A number of the plants collected by E.H. Wilson from the mountains of western China were sucessfully grown. Forrest, Farrer, Kingdon-Ward, Rock, Ludlow and Sherriff all supplied plants to Stern's garden and he discov-ered that most plants growing at 7,000-8,000 feet (2,100-2,400 metres) in China and Tibet would grow successfully in Britain. He will always be remembered for the blue poppy *Meconopsis betonicifolia*.

Top Places

PLAYING THE FIELDS

SPORTING SUSSEX

F ew parts of England have been more devoted to leisure than Sussex. Hunting was the earliest sport. The most ubiquitous hunting grounds were deer parks which increased rapidly from the 12th century with the introduction of fallow deer from the Near East. These were only obtained by licence from the Crown and soon became status symbols to distinguish a noble or a gentleman. The optimum shape of a deer park was circular or egg-shaped, giving a maximum internal area for the minimum of fencing. The average-sized park was some 100-150 acres (40-60 hectares).

It is an interesting exercise to examine the Ordnance Survey maps for spaces devoid of old farm buildings and other signs of settlement for this can often be regarded as prima-facie evidence for the possible site of a medieval deer park, especially if it has the tell-tale circular or oval shape. One such place is on the outskirts of Lindfield. Place names can also offer clues. The field walker should then investigate for signs of a pale, i.e. a prominent earth bank with a ditch on the outside to make the escape of deer more difficult. (This is the reverse of the conventional boundary bank which has a ditch placed on the inside.) Many medieval deer parks were enclosed directly from the wildwood and to this day old sites tend to contain relatively unmodified tree and plant habitats which elsewhere have been destroyed by farming. Moreover, many deer parks were subsequently embodied in the mania for landscaped parks from the 18th century and consequently many majestic trees have been saved from the forester's axe, as in Sheffield Park. Thus a walk around the perimeter, or inside, of a former deer park can be a most rewarding experience; you can admire the trees and shrubs and know that if the field walking is spot on you will return after a not-too-tiring walk to the starting point!

Hunting grounds also comprised forests and chases. Sussex had no less than five great medieval forests – St Leonard's, Worth, Ashdown, Waterdown and Dallington. They were originally Crown possessions and were not necessarily wooded for the word 'forest' was derived from the Latin *foris*, meaning 'out of the jurisdiction of the common law'. They were enclosed by a prominent earth bank – the pale – and this was of the same construction as that of a deer park. Deadwood or fencing was piled on top of the pale to complete the barrier. A chase was similarly devoted to hunting and, although nominally reserved for the king, was usually held by some magnate by the express grant of the Crown. Such hunting grounds ranged far and wide over the Sussex Weald up to the 16th century and as they were not fenced deer roamed freely and destroyed peasants' crops.

Ashdown Forest, which originally enclosed about 11,000 acres (4,500 hectares) of land, still partially retains the boundary pale which can be identified by walking. At intervals the pale was broken by deer-proof gates known as hatches. For administrative purposes the Forest was divided into three wards, each divided by earth banks. A number of majestic trees survive. Within the Forest rabbits, known as coneys, were introduced by the Normans and kept in warrens. These were enclosures on which long and narrow 'pillow mounds' were erected, typically up to 150 yards (137 metres) long, 6 feet (2 metres) high and 20 feet (6 metres) broad, into which rabbits burrowed into soft, dry soil and were taken out with the aid of a ferret by spreading a net along the side of the mound.

Much of the Sussex landscape has also been shaped by fox hunting over the past 200 years, as many surviving hedgerows, coverts, copses and neat field gates bear witness. To accommodate guests of the Charlton

Hunt, the second Duke of Richmond (1701-50) built accommodation and kennels on one side of the village street and a Palladian-style brick box called Fox Hall, now owned by the Landmark Trust who have restored the building and let it for self-catering holidays. The kennels at Goodwood House have only recently been cleared away to make room for the new golf course buildings. During the past 100 years much farmland has been turned over to pheasant shoots and this has involved much woodland planting.

The growth of golf

Golf became a popular sport at the end of the 19th century. The first three courses in the country were the Royal Eastbourne, Brighton and Hove and Seaford, opened in 1887; the Royal Ashdown Forest followed in the next year and Littlehampton in 1889. Rye Golf Club came into existence in 1893 on Camber Sands which offered the perfect conditions for links golf. Meanwhile other courses were multiplying and although initially golf was a male preserve, the growth of ladies' golf was to prove remarkable, and the Sussex County Ladies' Golf Association was founded in 1900. Golf courses quickly began to attract up-market housing, as at Ham Manor near Rustington. In the 1980s and 1990s the growth of interest in golf amongst a wider section of the public combined with the decline in agriculture has led to the setting up of many new courses. The rate of increase has since slowed down and a number of courses, notably on the west and poorly drained Weald Clay, have closed down. The overall effect was to remodel a substantial area of Sussex with the same intensity and rapidity as the earlier pleasure landscaping based on country houses (*see p.64 and p.68*).

Cricket's cradle

With Surrey and Kent, Sussex can claim to be a cradle of cricket. The earliest pitches were mainly in the triangle between Chichester, Midhurst and Arundel which had the springy turf the game needed. Cricket was being played at Sidlesham in 1611 and at Boxgrove in 1623; there is also early mention of the game at East Lavant, Midhurst and Arundel.

Under the patronage of the second Duke of Richmond, Slindon notably played London teams on the Artillery Grounds in London during the 18th century, the most famous player being Richard Newland.

Horse & courses

The diary of Thomas Marchant of Hurstpierpoint mentions horse-racing in 1718, at Shermanbury Place, Portslade and Lewes, and Thomas Turner, the diarist-shopkeeper of East Hoathly, twice attended the latter venue in the mid-18th century,when it was in the hands of the Pelham family who had established it before 1714. Lewes was eclipsed when racing at Brighton began during the Regency. It was then highly fashionable but went socially downhill when plagued by race gangs in the 1930s. Goodwood racecourse celebrated its second centenary in 2002. Fashionable crowds, including Edward VII, flocked to the event known as 'Glorious Goodwood' and with the new parade ring, distinctive stands and pavilion with elliptical canopies, the Goodwood course snaking its way through the Downs is probably the loveliest racecourse in Britain.

Aristocratic pursuits

Polo began at Cowdray Park in 1910 when the sport was started by the second Viscount Cowdray. The third Viscount revived it after World War II and Cowdray Park has become the home of British polo. Midhurst has become 'polo town' where people have grown used to seeing Argentinian gauchos shopping at the local superstore.

Shooting has been a major social institution since the end of the 19th century when the present driven shooting was introduced with the invention of the breech-loading gun from the 1860s. The breech-loader inspired the rearing of pheasants and invitations to weekend country-house parties for shoots between November and Christmas. As long as shooting persists, Sussex will retain its untidy but lovely woods.

Top Places

◗ *The Forest pale is traceable for some length near the course of the long-distance walking path, the Vanguard Way, at TQ490292 and north-west of Wych Cross at TQ397333*

◗ *The best remaining medieval deer park is at Eridge Old Park*

SUBURBAN SPRAWL

MODERN SUSSEX

It was the London to Brighton railway that brought the first modern development to Sussex. It created three new urban settlements along the line of the railway from late Victorian times – Haywards Heath, Burgess Hill and Hassocks – in the central Weald and suburban villas spread over the surrounding countryside. The destruction of natural beauty continued at a rate even before World War I. Brighton, for example, was surging up downland slopes by 1900 and threatening to engulf whole villages such as Preston and Patcham.

At the same time, Charles Neville was starting to build a 'rash of bungalows, houses, shops, shacks, chicken runs, huts and dog kennels' at Peacehaven by when the advent of the motor car was allowing a wider choice of settlement. Then, soon after the end of the war, a general inundation broke in. The South Downs and the coast were the worst affected and the indiscriminate defacement of some of the noblest scenery in England led to the creation of voluntary environmental bodies in the absence of strong control at both national and local government levels, such as the Society of Sussex Downsmen (now the South Downs Society) in 1923 and the Council for the Preservation of Rural England (now the Campaign to Protect Rural England) in 1926. Despite this, by 1936 the whole south coast of England from the South Foreland to Poole was by then practically one long suburb of London.

Brave new world

Haywards Heath divided people's opinions. M.A. Lower wrote approvingly in 1870 of the many villas and 'pleasure residences' that had sprung up like magic, but John Halsham, who lived at Lindfield nearby, likened the new town in 1898 to a 'congeries of stucco villas and builders' lots, nursery grounds and brickyards fenced with corrugated iron and barbed wire...'. Halsham was so moved that he was the first to advocate a National Park for the Weald and Downs. Residents of Haywards Heath still call it affectionately 'The Heath' although the common was enclosed in 1862 and has been obliterated.

Meanwhile the western High Weald between Horsham and East Grinstead, a district with fine views and rock outcrops, relatively cheap land and accessibility to London, was being colonised by newcomers who gothicised their country homes in the manner of French chateaux or 14th-century manor houses, or built a neo-Tudor or Georgian mansions. For two generations the villas were lively with laughter and song and the districts prosperous, as the many trim cottages, well-constructed farm buildings and carefully tended by-ways remind us. By 1939 villa building had ended and villas became an anachronistic survival until being taken over by a new breed of City person since the last war.

Up on the Downs

The unregulated spatter of buildings in the 1920s spread into Woodingdean near Brighton at 'Brighton Heights' on the edge of Brighton racecourse. Another potentially destructive proposal was for a new town to be called 'Newhaven on Sea' at Denton. More than 100 plots on downland were sold for dwellings, but fortunately only a small part of the scheme was realised. Other attempts at development were frustrated at Birling Gap, on the cliffed coast near Beachy Head. Between 1885 and the 1930s Carew Davies Gilbert, owner of about one third of Eastbourne, tried repeatedly to create a new resort there to be called 'Southdown Bay' complete with a railway extension and promenade. This collapsed with the reluctance of the railway company to build a line but, undaunted by opposition, in 1927 Gilbert began promoting a 'Motorists

Estate de Luxe' at nearby Crowlink which was forestalled by the intervention of Arthur Beckett of the Society of Sussex Downsmen and the National Trust.

Charles Neville's Peacehaven was to be the greatest centre of controversy. He bought large stretches of farmland for housing along the main road running along the cliff top between Newhaven and Rottingdean. Some of his work deserves praise, such the Arts-&-Crafts houses at Rottingdean in a mock-Tudor style and the Lido (1935) at Saltdean, now regarded as one of the finest Art Deco buildings in the country. Peacehaven, the earliest of Neville's creations, has been consistently reviled and derided, although not all have seen it as a national laughing stock.

Coastal explosion

Meanwhile the coast west of Brighton was also going under housing. Philip Gosse lamented in 1936 that it had been once a pleasant walk on the upper coast road (A 270) between Hove and Worthing but that bungalows and houses built all anyhow had turned him off. He found the same had happened west of Worthing where in Richard Jefferies' day (c.1900) fields ran down to the seashore. The modern development of Goring-by-Sea is representative of the urbanised coastline which also included, Angmering, Rustington, Middleton and Felpham. Fragments of the original small rural village of Goring are visible in thatched flint cottages and old flint walls formerly surrounding farmhouses and barns. Its 19th-century country houses survive only as institutions and commercial premises, although the magnificent holm oak avenue planted by the owners of Goring Hall remains a beautiful walk and a haven for wildlife.

The main catalyst for change was the absorption of Goring into the borough of Worthing in 1929, the advent of the motor car and the electrification of the railway to London in 1938. In 1901 the population had hardly increased from the 1801 level of 491; by 1991 it had reached 22,000. This illustrates the spate of pre- and post-war housing which overran the coastline. Little thought was given to the preservation of old buildings and over the past 50 years so many have been demolished that the identity of the village has been wholly lost in suburban sprawl. Here and there gaps were left in the general run of housing. At Ferring local people have vowed to defend it to their last breath. Similar emotions saved Cissbury Ring from lampposts and kerbstones in the 1930s.

The weekenders

One of the most important agency of change in Sussex was the habit of weekending by comfortably-off people. As we have noted (*see p.59*) rural cottages were coveted by others than cottagers a good many years before Jane Austen wrote about them as toys for a sunny day. Yet weekending did not become general until good railway services became available from the 1880s, and with the coming of the motor car it reached its zenith. Weekending in the country or at the seaside was not confined to Londoners; Brightonians also left the city periodically. The primary object of weekending was to recover simple living by 'roughing it' without servants, a habit that unfortunately displaced rural workers from their cottages.

Architecturally, holiday homes were being built in Sussex with labour-saving devices and such features as sliding glass windows and doors and new styles of interior decoration to take advantage of fresh sea or country air and sunlight. Leading modernists such as Chermayeff, Yorke, Bruer, Ward, Moro and Lucas overcame the resistance of local authorities and built in the style of Gropius and the Bauhaus, so introducing the true modern house – Bentley Wood at Halland, the Sun House at Chelwood Gate, and Sea Lane House at East Preston are examples. In utter contrast were the houses promulgated unashamedly for weekend occupation by R.F. Wells in the inter-war years at Storrington and West Chiltington which so faithfully imitated the Wealden hall houses of the 15th century that by the 1970s they were being passed off as the real thing.

Top Places

- Bentley Wood, near Halland, north of Lewes
- Harbour Meadow, Birdham, near Chichester, by Peter Moro
- A walk from the 'Flying Fish' public house up over the Downs to Denton
- The private estate of Aldwick near Bognor
- The East Dean Estate on the edge of the village of East Dean near Eastbourne

DEFENDING THE REALM

SUSSEX AT WAR

Owing to Sussex's location on the English Channel it has repeatedly been exposed to the threat of invasion and witnessed the embarkation of armies and fleets engaged against the enemy. Of Iron Age date are not only the hillforts but the great linear earthworks on the Downs such as the Chichester Dykes, the Devil's Dyke and the War Dyke. Sussex was possibly a prime target in the Roman invasion of AD 43 (*see p.22*) and fell prey to barbaric attacks in the 4th and 5th centuries. The Late Saxon period saw the founding of *burhs* as refuges against the Danes (*see p.30*) and the refortification of Cissbury Ring and Highdown. In 1066 the ravages of William the Conqueror's army were widespread and one of the scenes in the Bayeux Tapestry shows the first English civilian war victim depicted in art, a woman and her child fleeing from their burning house. In the 12th century the Knights Templar, based at Shipley, set sail from Shoreham for the Crusades. In 1264 Henry III lost the Battle of Lewes to Simon de Montfort during the Hundred Years War. Exceat at Cuckmere Haven was razed to the ground, at Rottingdean villagers were burnt to death in their parish church; other brutalities occurred, but no worse than Sussex men wrought on the French.

The Napoleonic Wars are marked by a number of landscape features. From Pett, near Hastings, the Royal Military Canal was dug across to Winchelsea and Rye and onwards across Romney Marsh into Kent. This was constructed to daunt Napoleon who threatened to invade England, but as William Cobbett remarked the dictator had crossed the Danube and was unlikely to be deterred by a 'mere ditch'. Beacon fires were set up on vantage points to signal his invasion, as numerous place names indicate. Between 1805 and 1812 the government strengthened the sea defences by building a chain of coastal emplacements known as Martello towers, shaped like upturned pots and inspired by French-built structures at Martella Point on the coast of Corsica. On flat open beaches on the south coast the Martellos were placed 600 yards (550 metres) apart and in total 74 towers were built between Folkestone and Seaford, with two circular redoubt forts at Dymchurch and Eastbourne acting as supply and control points. The inside was almost circular with walls up to 13 feet (4 metres) on the seaward side. On the first floor was accommodation for an officer and a garrison of 24 men. The ground floor housed provisions, ammunition and gunpowder. The upper floor was the gun platform. It was reasoned that an approaching enemy vessel would be fired upon from 15 Martellos before it reached the shore. The Wish Tower at Eastbourne has been restored and is open to the public and the Martello at Seaford is now the town's museum. At Pevensey and Norman's Bay two have been converted into residences.

Forts & foreign fields

In the 1850s Palmerston's forts at Littlehampton, Shoreham and Newhaven were built to counter another threat from France. These were known as redoubt forts where a garrison guarding an estuary would fire at different angles on the enemy and at a last resort rifle fire would greet an invader charging up the shingle. Shoreham's fort is sadly again in a state of disrepair but Newhaven's has been restored and is the site of a military museum.

One of the most remarkable recruiting achievements in World War I was that of Claude Lowther of Herstmonceux Castle, who was authorised to recruit a battalion of Sussex men for overseas service. His 'Southdowns' defended the area north and south of the Downs with pride and to join them and start initial training at Cooden Hill, before going to the Front, was the aspiration of every shopman and farm labourer, as this extract from their marching song indicates:

> ...*We have come from shop and sheepfold*
> *We have come from deck and store,*
> *We have left our peaceful callings*
> *To be taught the trade of war...*

Wartime Sussex

From the autumn of 1941 to early 1944 the defence of the Sussex coast was largely in the hands of the First Canadian Army. Officers were based at country houses such as Wiston House, near Steyning, from where General Montgomery directed the defence of the coast following Dunkirk. Other country houses such as Knepp Castle, Burton Park, Lavington House and Wakehurst Place housed English and Scottish troops. The Second Battalion of the Canadian Army suffered severe losses at Dieppe in August 1942 and each year there is a memorial service at Wisborough Green, which was one of the headquarters of the Canadian troops involved.

At the beginning of 1944 British troops were stationed in great secrecy in hotels at Worthing, embarking on June 6th at Gosport for the Normandy beaches. The Guards Armoured Division packed the Steine and surrounding streets at Brighton on the eve of D-Day and at the same time General Eisenhower stayed briefly at the Ship Hotel, Chichester, where a plaque records that RAF Tangmere, commanded by the South African veteran 'Sailor' Malan, honoured him with a dinner. Meanwhile the whole of the Downs east of Littlehampton had been requisitioned by the army for training in preparation for D-Day. Stanmer village and many farmhouses were so badly damaged by live ammunition that they had to be rebuilt after the war. The Kithurst military range was used by the 8th Infantry Brigade of the 3rd Division which led the assault on Sword Beach on D-Day. Near Chanctonbury Ring a Churchill tank has been dug up and put on view. A permanent legacy of wartime was the specially metalled roads up the crests to the Downs created by the military, such as Firle Beacon.

Wings over Sussex

RAF Tangmere and its satellites – Ford, Thorney, Westhamptnett (Goodwood) and Merston near Chichester were in the front line after Dunkirk through to the end of the war. Its aircraft were heavily engaged in northern France just before and during the allied attack. The airfield was equipped with Typhoon fighter bombers specially designed to strike enemy tanks. Tangmere remained operational until 1967. A memorial stone was erected by its legendary flier Douglas Bader and its lost airmen are buried in Tangmere church cemetery.

Five new airfields were constructed to give support to the D-Day landings – four in the Chichester area (Apuldram, Bognor, Selsey and Funtington) and one at Coolham, near Billingshurst. Funtington was for a time the base of Canadians led by 'Johnny' Johnson, whose total of 38 confirmed enemy aircraft shot down made him the highest scoring Allied fighter-pilot in the war. Shoreham Airport was mainly used for air-sea Rescue. Friston Airfield on the cliffs near Eastbourne also played its part in the war.

All over Sussex is evidence of military defences protecting the routes to London. After Dunkirk, civilian volunteers were recruited to sabotage key sites in the event of an enemy invasion. Tortington Manor was their regional HQ. Each patrol had an underground hide-out, not all of which have been recorded. Great secrecy surrounded this defence force, which would have been on a par with the French Resistance, and only now is information leaking out about it. Hundreds of pillboxes and other defences were hurriedly erected, most of which still survive in some form, as in the Cuckmere Valley.

Top Places

⊗ *Apuldram, near Chichester where there is a Spitfire in a garden*

⊗ *The Cuckmere Valley walk led by Bob Allen from the Seven Sisters Country Park to see wartime installations not noticeable to the unseeing eye*

⊗ *The Military Museum, Tangmere, established by enthusiasts, which houses wartime aircraft and other memorabilia of World War II*

THE TURN OF THE TIDE

THE SAVING OF THE COUNTY

For the survival of much of our beautiful countryside and townscape we are indebted to a movement which found utterance from the 1920s in the press, at public meetings and by the formation of voluntary societies for the preservation of natural beauty and the protection of historic buildings from the ravages of the jerry-builder. The pioneer in this regard was 'John Halsham' (G. Forrester Scott) who advocated what we now term a National Park for part of the Weald and Downs in 1898 and foresaw the countryside protection we are familiar with, but correctly prophesied that it would be too late.

By the late 1920s the tide of public opinion was turning against the speculative builder, so extensive was the damage to the environment from indiscriminate housing. With respect to the South Downs much public indignation went into saving them which appears to have been the driving force behind authorities' attempts to alleviate the damage. Arthur Beckett expressed this opinion in a landmark document, the *Report of the Regional Planning Scheme for Brighton and Hove District* (1932), the first of its kind to seek to preserve the natural beauty and character of the South Downs. The intention drew praise from local landowners in the area who added their own concerns.

A standard practice was for objectors to a development to send a letter to *The Times*, or another national newspaper, or to a weekly magazine such as *The Spectator*. The former, which took a strong stand against desecration published on Saturdays photographs of threatened sites, especially in the South Downs, where the picture editor, Ulric van den Bogaerde, Sir Dirk Bogarde's father, weekended with his family. It was letters to this newspaper that helped to save the cliffs at Fairlight in the neighbourhood of Hastings and put underground electricity cables in the unspoilt village of Amberley. The correspondence was initiated by that great fighter C.E.M. Joad in 1936. Joad was one of the most vociferous champions of the Sussex countryside. He attacked the 'outrages' committed at Newhaven, where he thought 'a venturesome people might even have sought to embellish the beauty of nature with the works of man', hammered away at the weekender and denounced the motorist. Kipling had earlier entered the fray with his verses *Too Many People* (1926), although it was the popularity of his Sussex works that was drawing people to the county.

Virginia and Leonard Woolf weekended and drove a motor car all over Sussex, but this did not prevent them lamenting the random development in their part of the Downs. In her diary, Virginia records all the fresh eyesores, whether houses, bungalows, shanties, or race-and-motor-cycle tracks and bursts into explosions of rage or despair, according to mood. Walter Wilkinson in his *Sussex Peep-Show* (1933) wrote of the cars that roared past his Punch and Judy show, 'Roar!, Rush!, Flash!' but although he warned of the great roads running through the county, he noted that along the little lanes you could still come upon a Sussex village which had not yet got into modern dress.

Parks & plans

Such expressions of opinion greatly bolstered the conservation movement. It led to Vaughan Cornish's vision for a National Park on part of the South Downs in 1929 and the West and East Sussex County Councils' collaboration with landowners which alleviated damage on the Downs after 1935. In the early post-war period the most devastating report on post-war planning came from the pen of Ian Nairn in 1955 who noted in his article 'Outrage' in the *Architectural Review* that the exigencies of the situation after the war had caused Brighton to ravage its downland some 5 miles (8 km) deep and 7 miles (11 km) wide. He denounced the 'visual hells' which doubly destroyed some of the noblest countryside and the original rural identity under subtopia.

A great setback two years later was the Government's decision not to proceed with a National Park for the South Downs on the grounds that too much of it had been ploughed since the declaration of war. Instead, after an agonising long interval, the Downs were made an Area of Outstanding Natural Beauty and the Weald was similarly protected later. AONBs are seen to have lesser status than National Parks because they do not have statutory administrative powers and financial resources. In addition, the management of AONBs is in the hands of local author-ities; no less than 15 local bodies are responsible for the protection of the South Downs and inevitably there are variations in competence, policies, commitment and resources.

In the early 1990s the demand for a National Park for the South Downs went unheeded but it led to a compromise, the setting up of a unique body, The Sussex Downs Conservation Board in 1992. This body has done admirable work. Its primary objective is to protect, conserve and enhance the natural beauty of the Downs. Its secondary objective is to promote quiet, informal, enjoyment of the Downs by the general public, to improve the relationship with farmers and landowners and other parties, and to foster the social and economic well-being of downland communities. It has solid achievements behind it, including a management plan for the whole of the Downs, but it has limited resources and has no secure and certain funding or future. In 2007 the Inspector holding the Public Inquiry on the South Downs recommended National Park status for the chalk country, saying that it deserved the additional resources that would accrue.

Top Places

◉ *Cuckmere Haven, the subject of controversial plans to transform its present character by allowing the sea to invade the existing defences*

◉ *The district of the western Weald north of Petworth and Midhurst which under current proposals (December 2007) has been rejected for National Park status*

CHANGE & CONSERVATION

SUSSEX TODAY

Since the last war Sussex has changed more rapidly and radically and with greater consequences than ever before. In 1945, for example, Crawley did not exist and Gatwick was a small grass airfield, the horse was still the main form of traction on many farms and mains water and electricity in many rural areas were still a dream. The economic changes have, for the most part, improved the standard of living generally but there are still people living in run-down parts of Hastings, Portslade and Fishersgate and in sleazy backstreets in Brighton, together with deprived rural areas such as the hinterland of Rye and Selsey and parts of Worthing, Littehampton and Bognor.

Crawley & Gatwick take off

Crawley was only a small town when designated as a New Town in 1947 to meet the requirements of the 1944 Greater London Plan to relieve overcrowding in the capital. A balanced and self-contained community of over 70,000 people has arisen against vociferous local opposition. The New Town was designed on the 'neighbourhood' principle, each neighbourhood having different types of housing in different proportions, so as to ensure a balanced community in each. These neighbourhoods were grouped in a double ring-road system and one industrial estate was provided. Crawley/Gatwick was later selected as the leading economic hub of the county; workers are currently earning the highest weekly wages in Sussex, two-thirds more than those at Hastings or Brighton, and the town has the fewest claimants for benefits.

Gatwick Airport began as a grass airfield in the 1920s, like Shoreham remains today. The 'Beehive' visible from the railway line was the original circular passenger terminal. It was requisitioned in the last war for the refurbishing of aircraft. In 1949 British European Airways began making short- haul flights to the Continent and in 1952 the Government announced its intention to develop Gatwick as an alternative to Heathrow. This entailed the diversion of the A23 road and a new railway station on the site of the old racecourse station. In 1988 the North Terminal was opened and Gatwick became the second largest British airport.

Beside the seaside

One of the most welcome changes for the better is the revival of the seaside towns. Hastings has won an award for the most improved seaside resort in England and the Master Plan for the town, in decline for 40 years, is intended to alleviate poor housing, bad transport, low average earnings and high unemployment with the creation of new sustainable communities and improved road access to London. Bexhill has accomplished the refurbishment of the iconic De La Warr Pavilion and this has coincided with the restoration of Wells Coates' 20th-century Embassy Court in Brighton. The towns of Worthing, Littlehampton and Bognor Regis, together with Selsey, have secured government funding to tackle restricted employment, low educational attainment and deprivation of the elderly. Littlehampton's rejuvenation is self evident. The decay of the harbour led to the running down of the East Bank which is now a mix of attractive homes, although retaining traditional building materials such as flint. The High Street is pedestrianised and shopkeepers have brightened up their shop fronts. At Shoreham-by-Sea, where the port has also declined, a prime waterside site abandoned 30 years ago has been refurbished with houses for 300 newcomers. Its shabby, hang-dog expression is changing now that fewer premises are vacant and nicer shops and restaurants have opened. A proposed development at the harbour of possibly 10,000 homes and 700 jobs with improved road and rail links is planned.

Restoring nature

A notable success in Sussex recently is the regeneration of natural habitats. Today heathland is rarer than rainforest so what remains of the Sussex heathland after the farming 'improvements' of the past two centuries is a national treasure. Ashdown Forest holds the largest expanse of this threatened habitat and one of the very few remaining stretches of lowland heath in Europe. There are also tracts in the Midhurst area and patches survive on the sandy soils at the foot of the South Downs, as at Sullington Warren. As grazing declined after World War I, the remaining heathland became covered with birch, scrub and rhododendron. The clock is now being put back by the Sussex Wildlife Trust, the National Trust and other organisations. Pines have been felled, rhododendron cut down and birches pulled up and bracken eradicated, to permit heather to regenerate. The aim of landscape architects is a mosaic which will create new viewpoints formerly obscured by trees and to open up a habitat for warblers, woodlarks, siskins, stonechats, nightjars and rare species of butterfly. Blackdown is now becoming more like it was when Tennyson and Victorian landscape painters knew it.

Another victory in conservation has been the saving of the Amberley Wildbrooks from intensive farming. With hindsight, this famous battle, which ended in favour of wetlands, turned the tide in their favour all over England. Locally it inspired the acquisition of the Pulborough Brooks by the Royal Society for the Protection of Birds which is managing them in the traditional way of seasonal flooding for birdlife. Meanwhile, Tony Whitbread and Susan Wilson of Sussex Wildlife Trust have drawn up an action plan to safeguard other Sussex water meadows and the creation of more marsh is a distinct possibility. Chalkland turf at present comprises less than two per cent of downland and it is very fragmentary but it is likely that attempts will be made to increase its extent and coherence.

The changing face of farming

It is extraordinary how great the farming revolution has been since 1939. Immediately after the declaration of war, the Government began the reclamation of derelict land abandoned in the 1930s. By the spring of 1942 the East Sussex War Agricultural Committee had reclaimed 8,000 acres (3,238 hectares) of former turf with the help of Fordson tractors and land girls. This presaged what was to be a watershed in the history of the Downs in the immediate post-war period. In exceptionally difficult times economically the Downs was transformed from its traditional mixed-farming 'sheep and corn' into a great industrial grain factory, ploughing up almost all the chalk turf and causing much destruction to archaeological monuments. In those gloomy and tumultuous early post-war years of austerity there was little chance of stirring public opinion environmentally. Quite forgotten then were the doughty defenders of the downland turf who had warned that its loss would be equivalent to the 'destruction of a priceless and unique manuscript'. It was not until 1954 that concerns about the widespread ploughing up of the Downs were reported in the public press, by which time the whole operation was unstoppable. It is only in recent years that attempts have been made to diversify the Downs and to offer inducements to farmers to practise more environmentally friendly farming.

In the Weald the changes worked differently. The small family farmer and the part-time farmer who supplemented his income by other means, the essence of the region since the medieval clearance of the woodland, sold out to bigger enterprises or, with their ancient farmhouses, to City people who usually turned the land over to 'horsey-culture'. Dairy farmers are now in danger of becoming an extinct breed.

The worst possible scenario was reserved for forestry and woodmanship, the blood and soul of the Weald. Commercial coppicing has virtually died out and forestry has greatly declined, yet four fifths of our timber is imported. This represents a great loss in employment and in intrinsic beauty and ecological interest, especially in coppice for without its regular cutting wild flowers and birds cannot take advantage of the periodic light. Such Wealden changes mean that, although the Weald looks much the same, the sudden decline in forestry and farming renders important landscape features such as woodland, hedgerows, pasture and ponds no longer fully functional, and this in the long term will have serious deleterious effects on the countryside. The High Weald AONB Management Plan, adopted in 2004, includes policies for protecting species-rich grassland, enhancing domestic timber production and protecting the historic pattern of settlement.

The future for Sussex

For almost the past 100 years slice after slice of green country has been urbanised. Throughout this book town and country have been treated as separate but if present trends continue the life of the countryside will be indistinguishable from that of towns. In numerous villages the traditional dwellers have been expelled, making once vibrant rural centres into chichi dormitories or places of retirement; farms have become theme parks or golf courses, and subtopia is spreading into the countryside like spilt treacle. Along the coastal edge of the Downs the familiar is depressingly unfamiliar producing something like the amorphous 'edge city' in America. Meanwhile all over Sussex the local distinctiveness which we once took for granted is being blurred by look-alike housing.

This reshaping of the landscape inevitably has brought into question whether Sussex can survive with a recognisable cultural identity. Hilaire Belloc in his *County of Sussex* (1936) doubted it and Desmond Sewell in his *Sussex* (1995) asked 'Does Sussex exist?' and replied that in many urbanised areas the only possible answer is 'No'. What will survive of the county's historic landscape and buildings in, say, 50 years' time? There is still so much in Sussex to be proud of. It remains a county of immense variety and surprises; many of its villages and small towns are amongst the most attractive in the country and much of its urban heritage has been saved. We must ensure that future change in Sussex is compatible with the centuries-old individuality and historical development which has made the county so distinctively beautiful and charming.

Top Places

- *Iping Common, near Midhurst, Blackdown and Ashdown Forest for heathland regeneration*
- *Ebernoe Common, near Petworth, managed by the Sussex Wildlife Trust, a fine example of a historic woodland common*
- *The Cowdray Estate, north of Midhurst, for forestry operations*

BIBLIOGRAPHY & FURTHER READING

Introduction

PETER BRANDON, *The Making of the Sussex Landscape*, Hodder and Stoughton Ltd, London, 1974

PETER BRANDON, *The South Downs*, Phillimore & Co, Chichester,1998

PETER BRANDON, *The Kent & Sussex Weald*, Phillimore & Co, Chichester, 2003

W.G. HOSKINS, *The Making of the English Landscape*, Hodder & Stoughton Ltd, London, 2005

A Geological Mosaic

HADRIAN ALLCROFT, *Downland Pathways*, Methuen, London, 1924

BRIAN DAWSON, *The Flint Buildings of West Sussex*, West Sussex County Council, Chichester, 1998

SHEILA KAYE-SMITH, *The Weald of Kent and Sussex*, Robert Hale, London, 1953

Taming the County

C. GREATOREX, 'Living on the margins? The Late Bronze Age landscape of the Willingdon Levels' in David Rudling (ed.), *The Archaeology of Sussex to AD 2000*, Heritage Marketing & Publications, Great Dunham, 2003, pp.89-100; plus various other authors pp.1-101

D. MCOMISH & P. TOPPING, 'The Archaeology of the South Downs',

in Gerald Smart & Peter Brandon (eds.), *The Future of the South Downs*, Packard Publishing, Chichester, 2007, pp. 32-41

PETER REYNOLDS, *Iron-age Farm: the Butser Experiment*, Colonnade/BM, London, 1979

Villas, Roads & Ruins

DAVID RUDLING, 'Roman Rural Settlement in Sussex: Continuity and Change' in *The Archaeology of Sussex to AD 2000*, Heritage Marketing & Publications, Great Dunham, 2003, pp.111-126

The South Saxons Arrive

PETER BRANDON, *The South Downs*, Phillimore & Co, Chichester, 1998, pp.58-62

M. GARDINER, 'Late Saxon Sussex, c. 650-1066', in Kim Leslie & Bryan Short (eds.), *An Historical Atlas of Sussex*, Phillimore & Co, Chichester, 1999, pp.30-31

D. HILL, 'The Origins of Saxon Towns' in Peter Brandon (ed.), *The South Saxons*, Phillimore & Co, Chichester, 1978, pp.174-189

William of Hastings

R. ALLEN BROWN (ed.), *The Normans*, St Martins Press, London, 1984

ELEANOR SEARLE, *Lordship and Community; Battle Abbey and its*

Banlieu 1066-1538, Pontifical Institute of Medieval Studies, Toronto, 1974

Ports in a Storm
HENRY CHEAL, *The Story of Shoreham*, Combridges, 1921
GRAHAM MAYHEW, *Tudor Rye*, University of Sussex, 1987

Making the Downs Work
F. ALDSWORTH, 'An Early Fifteenth-century Barn at Charlton Court, Steyning', *Sussex Archaeological Collections*, 145, Sussex Archaeological Society, 2007, pp.153-179
MARTIN BRUNNARIUS, *The Windmills of Sussex*, Phillimore & Co Ltd, Chichester, 1979
J. PENNINGTON & P. PLATTS, 'Deserted settlements 1066-1500' in Kim Leslie & Bryan Short (eds.), *An Historical Atlas of Sussex*, Phillimore & Co, Chichester, 1999, pp.48-49

Christian Sussex
ARTHUR PONSONBY, *The Priory and Manor of Lynchmere and Shulbrede*, Barnicott and Pearce, Shulbrede, 1920
SIR ANTHONY RICHARD WAGNER & ANTONY DALE, *The Wagners of Brighton*, Phillimore & Co Ltd, Chichester, 1983

Commerce & Castles
COLIN E. BRENT, *Georgian Lewes 1714-1830: The Heyday of a Country Town*, Colin Brent, Lewes, 1993

PETER JERROME, *Petworth: Time Out of Mind*, The Window Press, 1982
THOMAS SHARP, *Chichester*, Chichester Corporation, 1948

Working the Land
M. BESWICK, *Brick-Making in Sussex: a History and Gazetteer*, 2nd ed., Middleton Press, 1993
HENRY CLEERE & D.W. CROSSLEY, 2nd ed. Merton Priory Press Ltd, London, 1995
ALEC CLIFTON-TAYLOR, *Six More English Towns*, BBC Books, London, 1981
GEORGE HUGH KENYON, *The Glass Industry of the Weald*, Leicester University Press, 1967
ERNEST STRAKER, *Wealden Iron*, David & Charles Reprints, 1969

First Resorts
ANTONY DALE, *Fashionable Brighton, 1820-1860*, Country Life Ltd, London, 1947
EDMUND WILLIAM GILBERT, *Brighton: Old Ocean's Bauble*, Methuen, London, 1954
JOHN LOWERSON, *Victorian Sussex*, BBC Books, London, 1972
H.C. PORTER, *The History of Hove, Ancient and Modern, 1897*

The Country House
PETER BRANDON, 'Lost Country Houses' in *Sussex*, Robert Hale, London, 2006
B.M. COLLINS, *F.P. Hornung: A Memoir*, London, 1970
CHRISTOPHER ROWELL & MARTIN ROBBINS, *Uppark Restored*, National Trust, 1999

Nature Enhanced

WENDY HITCHMOUGH, *Arts and Crafts Gardens*, V & A Publications, London, 2005

DAVID JACQUES, *Georgian Gardens: The Reign of Nature*, Batsford, London, 1983

Playing the Fields

ROSEMARY BAIRD, *Goodwood – Art, Architecture, Sport and Family*, Frances Lincoln Publishers, London, 2007

LEONARD CANTOR (ed.), *The English Medieval Landscape*, University of Pennsylvania Press, Philadelphia, 1982

BARBARA WILLARD, *The Forest: Ashdown in East Sussex*, Sweethaws Press, 1993

Suburban Sprawl

PETER BRANDON & BRIAN SHORT, *South-East England from AD 1000*, Londman, London, 1990

PETER MERCER & DOUGLAS HOLLAND, *The Hunns Mere Pit: The Story of Woodingdean and Baldsdean*, Book Guild Ltd, Brighton, 1993

M. SMALL, 'Development Issues' [in the South Downs] in Gerald Smart & Peter Brandon (eds.), *The Future of the South Downs*, Packard Publishing, Chichester, 2007, pp.135-9

M.A. LOWER, *A Compendious History of Sussex, vols I & II*, W.J. Smith, Brighton, 1870

Defending the Realm

MARTIN BROWN, 'War and Rumour of War: The Defence of Sussex, 1530-1990' in David Rudling (ed.), *The Archaeology of Sussex to AD 2000*, Heritage Marketing & Publications, Great Dunham, 2003, pp.191-202

KEITH GRIEVES, *Sussex in the First World War*, Sussex Record Society, vol 84, 2000

The Turn of the Tide

P. BELDIN & A. TINGLEY, 'Establishing the Areas of Natural Beauty and their Management', in Gerald Smart & Peter Brandon (eds.), *The Future of the South Downs*, Packard Publishing, Chichester, 2007, pp.153-168

JOHN HALSHAM, *Idlehurst, A Journal Kept in the Country (1898)*, Kessinger Publishing, 2008

C.E.M. JOAD, *The Untutored Townsman's Invasion of the Country*, Faber, London, 1946

HENRY SMITH & PETER BRANDON, 'Is the South Downs National Park a good idea?', *Sussex Life*, September 2007, pp.98–101

Change & Conservation

GERALD SMART & PETER BRANDON (eds.), *The Future of the South Downs*, Packard Publishing, Chichester, 2007

SUSSEX DOWNS CONSERVATION BOARD, *A Management Strategy for the South Downs area of Outstanding Natural Beauty*, 1996 ed.

A Vision for the Wildlife of Sussex, Sussex Wildlife Trust, Henfield, 1996

INDEX